A PRAGMATIC THEORY
OF PUBLIC ART AND
ARCHITECTURE

PHILIP E. DAVIS

ISBN 10: 1511718668
ISBN 13: 9781511718660
Library of Congress Control Number: 2015906710
CreateSpace Independent Publishing Platform
North Charleston, South Carolina

CONTENTS

INTRODUCTION:

THE PERSPECTIVE OF PRAGMATISM

The word, pragmatism, is derived from the Greek word, *pragma,* which means action. Charles Sanders Peirce first introduced the term as a way of expressing his view that beliefs are really only rules for action, and that therefore in order to fully understand the meaning of our beliefs, we only need to consider what conceivable effects on conduct those beliefs (or rules) might have. Since Peirce's pronouncement, others such as William James, John Dewey, and a host of others have promoted pragmatism as essentially an epistemological method, the aim of which is to clarify our ideas and understand better what we mean by truth. The role of pragmatism in matters of morality, law, politics, education, and aesthetics was not initially given the attention it deserved. Meaning and verification held the primary spotlight and interest of professional philosophers for many decades.

However, the modern classical philosophers themselves, particularly James and Dewey, whom Morton G. White calls the "ur-pragmatists,"[1] were not unaware of these more normative and broader applications of pragmatic thought—broader in the sense of going beyond the narrower confines of Peirce's Principle. In fact they realized that if we go back in time before Peirce's profound insight, we can find pragmatism practiced by philosophers such as Socrates, Aristotle, and Kant. In response to the

---

1 White, *A Philosophy of Culture,* 125.

claim that justice is simply a matter of giving back to persons what belongs to them, Socrates, for example, asks whether it would be just to give back to a person a weapon he had entrusted to you, if that person was not then in his right mind. That is a clear application of pragmatic thought to a moral question. In a similar fashion, Aristotle's notion that a hand is not a hand except as a functional part of a living human body, and his theory of fourfold causes, one of which (the final cause) is purposeful—these are also akin to the pragmatic notions of organic unity and functionality. Dewey cites both of these notions in his book, *Experience and Nature*. Regarding the first in his chapter entitled "Experience, Nature and Art, (367-8) he says that the notion of "a working coordinated part of a balanced system of activities [such as a body] . . . applies to all things that are means;" and regarding the second he says, "The Aristotelian conception of four-fold 'causation' is openly borrowed from the arts" and so presumably relevant to any aesthetic discussion of them. Immanuel Kant, whom Peirce studied intensely, provided him with the notion of practical reason (and even the German term "pragmatisch"), which undergirds much modern pragmatic thinking about normative matters involving law, morality, religion, and aesthetics.

To speak of a "pragmatic perspective," however, is not to suggest that pragmatism is just another philosophy with distinctive dogmas of its own, or that different pragmatists never disagree with each other. As we shall see, and as William James repeatedly points out, pragmatism does not aim at producing a unique set of fundamental beliefs or tenets, but remains basically only a method as Peirce proposed it to be, but enlarged beyond epistemological concerns to become a more general procedure by which one belief, of whatever kind, might be judged superior to another. Unlike utilitarians, for instance, pragmatists do not suggest that the highest good human beings can or should attempt to achieve is the greatest happiness of the greatest number. Nor like Marxists do they all necessarily favor the achievement of a classless society. Rather they choose to await the outcome of social experiments in order to determine which action or policy is most conducive to the betterment of society.

Nor should it be thought that all pragmatists have exactly the same commitments regarding philosophical issues. They do on occasion disagree with one another. James for instance extended Peirce's Principle[2] to apply far beyond what Peirce himself had in mind. So outraged was Peirce that he considered changing the name of his philosophical viewpoint from "pragmatism" to "pragmaticism." There are times too, as we shall see, when Dewey disagrees with James or at least adopts somewhat different views.

It should not be particularly surprising to discover that pragmatists, in their own distinctive ways, differ from one another, especially if one considers the plethora of "neo-pragmatisms" which have sprung up in the last one hundred years. Thus we have seen "legal pragmatism" developed as an alternative to legal formalism, with its impetus from Justice Oliver Wendell Holmes; "holistic pragmatism" advanced by Morton G. White; the "post-philosophical pragmatism" of Richard Rorty; the "logical pragmatism" of Willard van Orman Quine (although he does not call it that);[3] the "conceptual pragmatism " of Clarence Irving Lewis; and the "idealistic pragmatism" as he himself called it of Josiah Royce (who is not usually associated with the pragmatic movement). Even Henry James, the novelist, claims to have adopted his brother's version of pragmatism, although it is a little unclear as to what distinguishes his "literary pragmatism."[4]

The point of citing all these neo-pragmatisms is to document the fact that although pragmatists do differ in the details of their thought, they still all retain the name of "pragmatism" by which to designate their specific brand of philosophical analysis. And so it seems reasonable to suppose that

---

2 According to Peirce in his article, "How to Make Our Ideas Clear," published in *Popular Science Monthly* (1878), the rule or principle is "Consider what effects which might conceivably have practical bearings we conceive the object of our conception to have. Then, our conception of these effects is the whole of our conception of the object." in H, S. Thayer, ed., *Pragmatism: The Classical Writings,* 88.

3 Morton White, a colleague of Quine at Harvard, has said, "Although Quine was a pragmatist and an empiricist in his approach to mathematics, logic, physics, and ontology, his pragmatism and empiricism virtually disappeared when he dealt with ethics." *A Philosophy of Culture,* 53.

4 Mark Twain also espoused what he called "ostensible philosophy," which appears to merit the name, "ostensible pragmatism" or "negative pragmatism." For a discussion of his views, see Davis, *Comparative Philosophy: Four Philosophical Americans,* 76, 177, 189, n.15.

despite their differences and disagreements there must be something they all have in common.

In this book what they share is what I have called "the pragmatic perspective." Here briefly is what I perceive that viewpoint, or perhaps more accurately, that commitment, to be. Of course the full elaboration of it will have to await its exhibition and application in later chapters, but it may be helpful to the uninitiated to provide a few hints of what it is all about. First let us consider its general character, and then how it applies specifically to our main subject of public art and architecture.

William James dedicated his book, *Pragmatism,* to John Stuart Mill from whom he says he "first learned the pragmatic openness of mind." Open-mindedness appears to be the first commitment of a pragmatist. He or she is willing to entertain unconventional and foreign ideas, and as Socrates advised, "to follow the argument where it leads." The second commitment is to the idea that the primary reality which philosophers need to investigate is human experience, not some Platonic heaven of ideas or some Kantian other-worldly noumenal reality. And what is most deserving of our attention in this world of sense are human actions. It is they in whom we live, move, and have our being. One of James' persistent criticisms of his brother's novels is that they lack "heartiness" and need either "picturesque elements of some sort or much action," all of which appears to be a typical reaction of a pragmatist devoted to the understanding of human life and conduct.

Pragmatism is not only empirically oriented (Dewey speaks of his philosophy as a "metaphysics of experience"), but also consequentialist and futuristic in its purview. The consequentialism derives not so much from utilitarian thought, with which it is closely allied but not identical with, but from an implication of Peirce's Principle which requires that in order to gain clarity for our ideas we must try to conceive all the possible future practical effects of our conceptions.

Finally, the pragmatist regards himself as an integral part of nature and not inherently or externally opposed to it, as some more theologically minded persons would have it. In practically all of his major works John

Dewey, for example, makes a point of insisting that human nature is a part of the natural world (cf. *Experience and Nature); that* human beings are "living creatures" (cf. *Art As Experience*); and that no fixed, i.e. absolute, distinction exists between the human [world] and the physical [world] (cf. *Human Nature and Conduct*). Most pragmatists, in short, are thorough-going environmentalists.

In matters involving art and architecture, particularly *public* art and architecture, a distinction which will be made clearer in our first chapter (which, incidentally, is quite in keeping with Peirce's efforts to make our ideas clear), pragmatists tend to favor environmentally friendly art, such as Jefferson's home at *Monticello* and Frank Lloyd Wright's *Fallingwater*. These artworks have been deliberately built into their specific surroundings and natural environments, as contrasted with buildings such as the Gothic cathedrals of earlier centuries with their poorly lit gloomy interiors, situated in the midst of soot- filled[5] cities.

Although pragmatists in aesthetics and indeed in other fields such as law and politics eschew strict formalism, i.e., a reduction of problems merely to the application of rules, most pragmatists, especially John Dewey but excluding Richard Rorty, insist that attempts to dispose of all rules as guides in decisional and creative processes is wrong. Dewey even castigates them as "the height of foolishness."[6] However, pragmatists tend to regard rules not as absolute and rational edicts, but more as empirical general-izations which are subject to change as our understanding of the natural world develops. In short, they are empiricists, not rationalists of the "pur-ist" variety such as Immanuel Kant in the areas of morality and law or Clive Bell in aesthetics, although as we shall see both of these philosophers have much of importance to say about art generally, about the capacity for aesthetic judgment, and about the aesthetic experience.

Functionality is also a component of the pragmatic perspective, espe-cially as it pertains to art. Just as Aristotle claimed that a hand severed from the human body is not really a hand but only a mass of flesh and bone, so

---

5 James uses the unusual but strikingly accurate term, "fuliginous." Above, 114.
6 Dewey, above, 126.

pragmatists are inclined to treat objects which lack a function as art objects. Thomas Jefferson, as we shall see, was very explicit on this point. He despised machines which failed to work as intended, and even disciplines such as metaphysics and historical geology which, in his opinion, served no useful purpose or provided no useful knowledge. Similarly, he thought the Lunatic Asylum at Williamsburg, Virginia, in the 18th century, resembled more a brick kiln than a hospital, and a facility in which the inmates were treated more like prisoners than patients. It was, he thought, an example of what architecture should not be; it was in fact an example of non-art. Like most pragmatists he was a functionalist.

In the chapters to follow, all of these characteristics of the pragmatic perspective will be discussed and illustrated in far greater detail, particularly as they pertain to the specific domain of public art and architecture.

Chapter I

WHAT IS PUBLIC ART?

Public art has existed for centuries, perhaps since the first caveman drew pictures on the walls of his cave. Some might claim that all art even today is "public" in some sense. But the variety of artistic productions has become so great—from crude paintings, drawings, and sculptures to monuments, buildings, parks, landscapes, and wind farms, as well as less material entities produced by human agency, such as ceremonial dances, political and military parades, civic ceremonies, patriotic celebrations and political rallies and events—that it is becoming nearly impossible to deny a distinction between the kind of art we experience in museums and artistic achievements of a more outdoors or dynamic character. Yet we still have difficulty drawing a definitive line between the two, For example, how are we to distinguish Michelangelo's *David* as a statue originally erected in a public square, the *Palazzo della Signoria*, outside the seat of civil government in Florence, Italy, where it served a political purpose, from the *David* as now installed in the same city, for protection from vandals and the elements, in the *Galleria dell'Accademia*, where it serves an academic purpose. Or does it still serve both purposes?

Perhaps no rigid distinction can be made. But consider another case, namely the Presidential faces carved on Mount Rushmore in the Black Hills of South Dakota and the paintings of Pierre Auguste Renoir in the Louvre in Paris. Here there does seem to be a vast difference in kind.

Indeed, when we include in our considerations the patriotic or other community related celebrations and ceremonies, or the interactive art creations such as the artistic water fountains that can be played almost like a piano by striking certain keys which selectively block the water flowing through different water jets[1] or other such "public works," and compare them to traditional "art works," there does seem to be a difference which is very present and difficult to ignore.

The terminology we used to discuss Michelangelo's *David*, namely civic (or public) versus academic (or non-public), however, really doesn't fit all the cases, particularly in the non-public category. Yet the logically all inclusive distinction of "public" versus "non-public" is not specific enough and consequently not very illuminating. Must we fall back on the natural antonym for "public" which of course is "private"? But that distinction has its difficulties too. It suggests a distinction based on ownership, on whether the public or some individual owns the art object, but that is not the issue we are concerned with here. [2]

For want of a better term, or pair of terms, for public and non-public, public and private, or civic and academic, let us examine a distinction often used by philosophers to describe different kinds of value, the distinction between "extrinsic," on the one hand, and "intrinsic," on the other, and see where it leads us.

Some object, act, or process has extrinsic value if its value or virtue is dependent upon something exterior to itself. It has intrinsic value if its value is independent of its site, setting, origin, or even the means of its creation. Thus a coin or a paper bill or note may have value only in relation to some system of exchange or currency, and little or no value in itself, and so it is said to have only extrinsic value. On the other hand, a painting by Rembrandt, regardless of where, why, or even how it was produced is totally irrelevant with respect to its aesthetic value which is wholly contained

---

1 See *Wikipedia*, "Public Art." These interactive musical fountains can be found in Ontario, Canada, and Melbourne, Australia.

2 In this connection there is a problem regarding the "privatizing" of public art, but it will be dealt with later.

within the object itself. To be sure, the "provenance"[3] of a painting is always relevant as far as determining what its economic value may be, that is, what its worth is in monetary terms, but strictly irrelevant as far as its aesthetic value is concerned. And so its value is primarily intrinsic in character.

Applying this distinction to our question about public art generally, it would seem that most of the objects, actions, or processes which we tend to look upon as "public art," such as sculptures, statues, monuments, bridges, parades, etc., appear to fall into the category of "extrinsic art." Their value as aesthetic creations are dependent upon a great many things quite exterior to themselves. For example, the Golden Gate Bridge in San Francisco Harbor couldn't look the way it does, e.g., having a 4200 foot long span, if the Bay and its shores weren't situated as they are. The bridge has been called the most beautiful bridge in the world, which may very well be an exaggeration, but it does suggest that it has aesthetic value though primarily of the extrinsic kind.

Many other examples of public art are declared by their creators to be "site specific." Perhaps the most notorious of these attempts at what has also been called "environmental art" are the efforts by Christo (Javacheff) of Bulgaria to wrap (with the assistance of his wife Jeanne-Claude) in colorful fabric just about every kind of thing in the world including rivers, mountains, a park full of trees, the German Reichstag building in Berlin and the Pont Neuf in Paris. Cristo has also been known to run an enormous curtain through a valley, wrap a coastline, locate hundreds of large umbrellas in the mountains of China (reminiscent of Andy Warhol's painting of a multiplicity of Campbell Soup Cans) and to create with fabric a miles-long fence which literally serves no useful purpose. His work with that of his wife also includes similar on-site "sculptures" inside buildings and museums as well as outside them. All of his works are of course very temporary in duration and while extant totally inseparable from their specific sites and locations.

---

3 *Provenance* [F] meaning source or origin, or *provenience* [E], literally from [L] *provenire,* to come forth.

Another case of "site-specific" as well as site-sensitive art is Richard Serra's 1989 artistic reorganization of Manhattan's Federal Plaza which he called "Tilted Arc." It was commissioned by the city's Art-in-Architecture Program. Unfortunately the office workers in the area found that the barriers he constructed interfered with their work habits involving traversing the Plaza and eating lunch there. Their complaints were heard by the Arts Commission and certain political leaders and it was suggested that "Tilted Arc" be moved to another plaza. The artist objected on the ground that the work was site-specific and that moving it to another site would utterly destroy the art he had created.

No such site-specific or site-sensitive claims are made for "intrinsic art." Take Leonardo da Vinci's *Mona Lisa*. Until after his death it did not even have a "home." Da Vinci carefully carried it about with him wherever he went. It now resides in the Louvre, but even if it were permanently located in the National Gallery of Art in Washington, D.C., as it once was temporarily, or the Minneapolis Institute of Art, it would still retain its aesthetic value wholly independent of those sites. Would it matter as far as our aesthetic appreciation of it is concerned if it were actually painted by someone else? I think not. Even well executed fakes of Johannes Vermeer's paintings are held in the highest regard.

Still we tend to cling to the notion that the provenance of a work of art and its mode of production are all important factors in judging its aesthetic excellence and in determining, to use another highly ambiguous and useless categorization, whether it is "fine art" or not. We are also constantly nagged by the notion that most art can under some circumstances have both kinds of value, intrinsic but also extrinsic value. Is that a contradiction?

In the strict sense in which we have been using the terms, intrinsic and extrinsic, which is also the usual way in which they have been defined, it is a contradiction. An object or act cannot be both totally dependent for its value on something external to itself and totally independent of such things. From the standpoint of the philosophy of pragmatism, however, such a dualism, like many others, is highly questionable and should be rejected or at least qualified. John Dewey is renown for his rejection of dualism in philosophy. Arthur Lovejoy has even written a book entitled, *The Revolt Against Dualism*. It is a position to be found in Charles S. Peirce's philosophy of synechism which stresses the continuity and interpenetration of concepts and percepts; and also in William James' concept of consciousness and the self which, unlike Descartes' theory of the mind as a distinct substance, treats mind as a "function" within our experience, such that at times some parts of our experience are "subjects" and at other times "objects." Dewey is wholesale in his rejection of philosophical dualisms. He thinks of means and ends as parts of a continuum, and speaks of means as modified by ends and ends or purposes as modified by the means we use to achieve those ends. He deals similarly with the classic distinctions between "mental" and "physical," "mind" and "body," "truth" and "falsity," "good" and "evil," and "right" and "wrong." He rejects all rigid definitions of these opposite terms including a rigid distinction between "art" and "craft."

It is quite clear that all these pragmatists would reject a distinction between "public" and "non-public" art and architecture which is based on the distinction between extrinsic and intrinsic value, at least so far as it is defined in terms of dependency on exterior objects or circumstances. They would *not* simply reject the distinction between public and non-public, any more than they would attempt to deny the distinction between mind and body, or means from ends. But they do insist on treating all these matters in terms of different functions, and consequently they avoid any contradiction in asserting that the same work of art might have separate functions. This consequence was indeed hinted at in our discussion of Michelangelo's *David*. There is nothing inconsistent in saying that it could function to promote political purposes (promoting heroic resistance to tyranny either of Goliath in Biblical times or of the Medici family in Florence, Italy) and an educational one by enlightening viewers and students not only about great sculpture but also about the male human body.[4] It matters not that

---

4 Many a viewer has wondered why Michelangelo made David's hands so large and seemingly out of proportion to the rest of his body. Some have suggested that it had to do with perspective, others with emphasizing the political power needed to overcome tyranny, and still others that Michelangelo was merely documenting the fact that some men have big hands.

the statue no longer serves a political purpose since both Goliath and the Medici are long gone, because even in the 16th century it also had an "academic' or educational aspect.

But suppose we adopt this more functional way of viewing art and architecture which allows that public art might serve some of the ends which so-called "fine art" also serves, and conversely that some non-public art may also serve some of the same purposes as public art, e.g. Picasso's "Guernica." The question still remains, Why do we habitually select statuary, buildings, monuments, and the like as public art and works such as portraits, landscape drawings, paintings, and interior decorations as non-public? The answer seems to be that it depends on whom the art and/or architecture[5] is directed towards. In the case of public art the persons aimed at are "The People." The Statue of Liberty was a gift to the People of the United States from the People of France; the Golden Gate Bridge was constructed primarily for and by the People of California; the Civil War military statues in the southern United States (all facing the South) are directed toward the People in the Confederate States. No such designations of audiences or viewers are targeted by intrinsic or "fine" art.

This difference is no mere accident of fortune or cleverly devised intention on the part of the artists involved. Art which is aimed at the People is art based on a profound sense of place.[6] Daniel Kemmis has insightfully pointed out and demonstrated that the phrase "We the People" in the *United States Constitution* is but the Founders' way of referring to the entire Republic and its place in the world, and similarly for the *Constitution of the State of Montana* which begins "We the People of the State of *Montana*, grateful to God for the quiet beauty of our state, *the grandeur of its mountains, the vastness of its rolling plains*, and desiring to secure to ourselves and our posterity the blessings of liberty for this and future generations,

---

5 I do not mean to juxtapose art and architecture in any absolute way, since the latter is clearly as much art as any other, but it is a separate art having somewhat different rules and a history of development which is distinct from the history of other kinds of art, if indeed they can be said to have a history at all. Cf. R. G. Collingwood, who says that "there is no history of artistic problems, as there is a history of scientific or philosophical problems. There is only the history of artistic achievements." *The Idea of History*, 314. More on this topic later.

6 For more on this aspect of these references, see Davis, *The Philosophy of Place*.

do ordain and establish this constitution."[7] The Constitution which John Adams originally wrote for the Commonwealth of Massachusetts similarly begins with "We, therefore, the people of *Massachusetts* . . ." The upshot of all these references to places in political and almost all other legal documents is that, as Tip O'Neil, former Speaker of the U.S. House of Representatives, put it, "all politics is local." If this be so, then all art which is so directed must also be "local." Thus we might perhaps more accurately describe "public" art in this sense as "local" art, i.e., the art of some place or other.

The contrast with non-public art can now be seen in a somewhat different light. No non-public art in the sense just described is "local." A Rembrandt painting or a Michelangelo statue is tied to no particular part of this physical universe. It is what it is quite apart from its setting. Not so public art. Thus, it is quite appropriate to designate the Golden Gate Bridge as *American* art, or the Statute of Liberty as *French* art, or Frank Lloyd Wright's *Fallingwater* architectural achievement in Pennsylvania as *American* art, but it seems a bit odd (though frequently done) to call Michelangelo's artistic creations, *Italian*, or Rembrandt's as *Dutch*. There is of course no oddity in calling Michelangelo, the artist, Italian, or Rembrandt, Dutch, but their artistic works are not easily or properly "localized" in that way.

Viewing public art, then, as directed primarily to "The People," and as a consequence to some particular place, having primarily only extrinsic aesthetic value, but to a limited degree also intrinsic value, we need also to realize that public art can also be judged as good or bad art, and indeed it has been. For example, one of the more infamous instances of allegedly bad public art is John Seward Johnson, Jr.'s twenty-six foot tall fiberglass statue of Marilyn Monroe replicating the scene in her 1955 movie "The Seven Years Itch" in which a burst of air raises her skirt showing her panties for all to see. It is tall enough so that adult persons can walk beneath the skirt and between her legs. The statue is called "Forever Marilyn" and was first erected in 1996 in the Pioneer Court near the Chicago Tribune

---

7 Daniel Kemmis, *Community and the Politics of Place*, 3-4.

Tower on the so-called "Magnificent Mile" of Michigan Avenue. In fact the court in which it was originally placed is privately owned by the Zeller Realty Group, and so, contrary to the usual practice of putting public art on government land, it is an example of public art exhibited on private land owned by a private company.

This sort of "privatization" of public art has raised some serious questions. For example, if the art is truly public, i.e., aimed at The People, shouldn't the people have some right to dictate its content, message, or moral demeanor? Doesn't this blurring of the distinction between public and private give too much power to corporate interests to influence political views, social prejudices, or buying habits? Might it not be used to deprive the poor, disadvantaged, the downtrodden, and down-market persons of their equal status in a democracy by effectively excluding such persons in some circumstances from such publicly used private property? These and other such questions will be discussed more thoroughly in our chapter on political art.

The "Forever Marilyn" sculpture has also been cited as an example not only of bad taste and kitsch, but of being morally offensive. A replica in China was discarded in a garbage dump. Others who have viewed the sculpture, which has since been moved in 2012 to a location in Palm Springs, California, have been somewhat more lenient in their assessment of its aesthetic value, and have found it interesting and a source of great amusement.

The next inevitable question is, how do we decide, or rather, how *should* we decide which public art is good and which is bad? I suppose that someone could take the position that art is value-neutral, perhaps consisting only as a matter of taste, not of reason, and so neither good nor bad. As the old adage goes, *De gustibus non est disputandum* (or "Regarding tastes there is no disputing")—the so-called "de gustibus principle." And one can always conduct a poll and find out, e.g., how many persons find "Forever Marilyn" objectionable or bad art, or how many persons think Christo's site-specific art absurd or simply silly. But that is to assume that art is essentially irrational and wholly relative to individual tastes, or to the preferences, likes or dislikes, of the masses, whether educated or not, and that art is ultimately beyond rational argument and discussion. Rarely does it make sense, however, to try to decide value questions by counting heads, and indeed, such issues are regularly and quite naturally argued and discussed, so the irrationalist view is definitely in defiance of common practice.

The same sort of claim has of course been made with respect to matters of morality. But it can easily be shown that that sort of relativism in moral matters is self-defeating. If one's moral standards, or conceptions of what is right, are as good as everyone else's, then it seems to follow that one's own standards are no better than anyone else's. Also if one's standards prove too difficult to follow in a consistent manner, there is nothing wrongful, according to this view, in adopting lower standards which are easier to follow, or indeed, to have any standards at all. If, as part of my moral code, if I have one, it is wrong to harm innocent persons, that view gives me no ground to suppose that others will agree and refrain from harming me. But this is not the place to discuss such relativistic views in greater detail. Since many very intelligent persons and philosophers have held that art does have objective standards, it seems reasonable to seek out what they could be. We shall first attempt to discover what Jefferson thought they were, at least with respect to architecture, which he frequently refers to as "this elegant and useful art."

Chapter II

WHAT IS THE DIFFERENCE BETWEEN GOOD ART, BAD ART, AND NON-ART?

Thomas Jefferson was highly critical of the architecture of his day. Partly for economic reasons many of the so-called "vernacular" buildings in early America were wood framed, clapboard homes much like his birthplace in Shadwell, Virginia, reportedly was, and as the Peyton Randolph House in Historic Williamsburg still is. In Jefferson's opinion, the "happiest" feature of such buildings is their perishability by fire.[1] Public buildings were built of stone or bricks, but the only ones worth mentioning, he reports in his *Notes on the State of Virginia,* are the Capitol, the [Governor's] Palace, which was his residence during his two year revolutionary war governorship, the College [William and Mary], and the Hospital for Lunatics, all in Williamsburg.[2] Regarding the College and the Hospital, he says, they "are rude, misshapen piles, which, but that they have roofs, would be taken for brick kilns."[3] It is a little surprising that his description of the College [presumably the so-called Wren Building] should have received such harsh criticism, since Sir Christopher Wren (1632-1723), who may or may not have designed the building, is one of those responsible for the second

---

1 Jefferson, *Notes on the State of Virginia,* 152.
2 Keep in mind that at this time none of the monumental buildings in Washington, D. C. were in existence.
3 *Notes,* 153.

11

revival of English Palladianism in the early 18ᵗʰ century.[4] Jefferson himself once proclaimed that as far as architecture goes, "Palladio is the Bible."[5] But even after viewing Palladian structures in Britain on his tour with John Adams in 1786, he remained critical of Wren's and Lord Burlington's attempts[6] to revive the style of Andrea Palladio (1508-1580). Both the Capitol at Williamsburg and the Governor's Palace were in that general tradition, although it must be said that the capitol Jefferson knew so well and criticized was the second Capitol built in 1783 after the first burned down in 1747.[7] So by the way, did the original Palace in 1781, and the original Hospital in 1885. The Wren Building sustained three major fires in 1705, 1859, and 1862.

Obviously in the eighteenth and nineteenth centuries American brick construction was no guarantee against destruction by fire, although it may have had other advantages. Indeed Jefferson was much concerned to refute the common view held then that wood construction was healthier than brick or stone. As he says,

> Architecture being one of the fine arts, and as such within the department of a professor of the college [William and Mary] . . .perhaps a spark may fall on some young subjects of natural taste, kindle up their genius, and produce a reformation in this elegant and useful art. But all we shall do in this way will produce no permanent improvement to our country, while the unhappy prejudice prevails that houses of brick or stone are less wholesome than those of wood.[8]

He goes on to "prove the errors" of this way of thinking. Estimating the average life of a wooden building at 50 years, he says,

---

4 Cf. Jack McLaughlin, *Jefferson and Monticello: The Biography of a Builder,* 55.
5 Ibid., 54, Isaac Coles to John Hartwell Cocke, Feb. 23, 1816, recounting a conversation he had with TJ.
6 Cf. James Stevens Curl, *A Dictionary of Architecture,* See **Burlington and Palladianism.**
7 McLaughlin, 59.
8 Jefferson, *Notes,* 153.

Every half century then our country becomes a *tabula rasa*, whereon we have to set out anew, as in the first moment of seating it. Whereas when buildings are of durable materials, every new edifice is an actual and permanent acquisition to the state, adding its value as well as its ornament.[9]

But even some brick structures do not measure up to Jefferson's (and Palladio's) standards. His specific criticisms of the [second] Capitol Building in Williamsburg, and his evaluation of the Governor's Palace are as follows:

> The Capitol is a light and airy structure, with a portico in front of two orders, the lower of which, being Doric, is tolerably just in its proportions and ornaments, save only that the intercolonnations are too large. The upper is Ionic, much too small for that on which it is mounted, its ornaments not proper to the order, nor proportioned within themselves. It is crowned with a pediment, which is too high for its span. Yet on the whole, it is the most pleasing piece of architecture we have. The Palace is not handsome without: but it is spacious within, is prettily situated, and with the grounds annexed to it, is capable of being made an elegant seat [of government].[10]

Jefferson's last statement reveals two aspects of his theory of architecture. First regarding the relation of architecture to gardening, he says that the Palace is "prettily situated, and with the grounds annexed to it, is capable of being made an elegant seat." Like Francis Bacon, one of his favorite philosophers, he agreed that gardens are "the greatest refreshment to the spirits of man; without which buildings and palaces are but gross handyworks."[11] Echoing both Bacon's admiration for gardens and no doubt also the account

---

9 Jefferson, *Notes*, 154.
10 Ibid., 152-3.
11 Francis Bacon, *Essays and the New Atlantis,* ed. Gordon S. Haight, 190.

in *Genesis* (2: 8-9) of the first garden "eastward of Eden," is Jefferson's description of the perfect garden:

> I have often thought that if heaven had given me choice of my position and calling, it should have been on a rich spot of earth well watered, and near a good market for the productions of the garden. No occupation is so delightful to me as the culture of the earth, and no culture comparable to that of the garden.[12]

Monticello was Jefferson's "Eden of the United States."[13] In his famous letter to Maria Cosway, he is even more poetic:

> And my own dear Monticello, where has nature spread so rich a mantle under the eye? mountains, forests, rocks, rivers. With what majesty do we there ride above the storms? How sublime to look down into the workhouse of nature, to see her clouds, hail, snow, rain, thunder, all fabricated at our feet! and the glorious sun when shining as if out of a distant water, just gilding the tops of the mountains and giving life to all nature.[14]

The second revelation in Jefferson's criticism of the Governor's Palace is his commitment to Palladio's rules and principles. He believed that Palladio's had enunciated once and for all the laws of order and symmetry in his *I Quattro Libri dell' Architettura* (1570). Before he discovered Palladio, Jefferson maintained that in Virginia "the first principles of [the elegant and useful] art are unknown, and there exists scarcely a model among us sufficiently chaste to give us any idea of them."[15] Even the Capitol was "insufficiently chaste" because of its serious departures from the norms

---

12 *TJ to Charles Willson Peale,* Aug. 20, 1811. Peterson, 1249.
13 *TJ to C. F. de C. Volney,* Apr. 9, 1797.
14 *TJ to Maria Cosway,* Oct. 12, 1786, *PTJ,* X, 443-53, Peterson, 870.
15 *Notes,* 153.

set by Palladio. As Jack McLaughlin has put it, "When he discovered the *Four Books* and compared the Capitol's flawed double portico with those of Palladio, he may have determined that he could do it much better. And he did. The orders he designed for Monticello are painstaking examples of Palladian orthodoxy."[16] Jefferson judged English Palladianism in the same manner: "Their architecture is in the most wretched style I ever saw, not meaning to except America where it is bad, nor here in Virginia, where it is worse than any other part of America that I have seen."[17]

But if Jefferson assumes, as he does, that the art of architecture is distinguished from non-art by being an activity or product governed by the Palladian rules (of symmetry, order, and proportionality), the question arises, are gardens and buildings which violate those rules (1) not fine or beautiful art,[18] but some lower class or degree of art; (2) really bad or "unchaste" art; or (3) simply not art at all? Jefferson believed, as McLaughlin aptly put it, that "if a building was designed according to the rule, it was not only beautiful, it was right."[19] The Capitol was not exactly right, but he says "it is the most pleasing piece of architecture we have." Does this claim contradict his view that in order to be beautiful the building must accord with Palladian rules? Not necessarily. There are apparently degrees of beauty or aesthetic value. The Capitol is not absolutely beautiful, but it is the *most* beautiful or pleasing piece of architecture extant in Williamsburg at that time.

Would a totally wretched building, e.g., the Hospital for Lunatics, which he thought resembled a brick kiln, be regarded as "bad art" or "no art at all"? Jefferson is not altogether clear on this point. The suspicion is that his answer to this question would depend on the building's function.

---

16 McLaughlin, 60.

17 Quoted in W.H. Adams, 23.

18 Some persons might object to the identification of "fine art" with "beautiful art." Jefferson himself seems to have no difficulty with it. He speaks of both architecture and gardening as "fine arts," the latter because of its association with another fine art, namely, landscape painting. Architecture he constantly refers to as "this elegant and useful art." The burden is perhaps on the one who wishes to contend that some works of art (other than craft) could be fine but not beautiful or beautiful but not fine art.

19 McLaughlin, 54.

Mere beauty (or ornament) apart from function was, for Jefferson, in architecture an abstraction, just as truth and morality apart from utility also were. A machine which failed in its function or a discipline such as metaphysics or historical geology which provided no guide to human conduct were "not worth a single hour of any man's life."[20] Art or architecture which lacks a practical function or only poorly performs would not have an appreciative audience in Jefferson. Thus with regard to his example of the Lunatic Asylum, which appears today to viewers as more of a jail than a hospital, he might have viewed it as bad architecture if at least it had a function. But if like Patrick Henry, who refused to commit his insane wife Sarah to that asylum for fear that they might not treat her properly,[21] he might regard it as no more functional than metaphysics or geology or a broken piece of machinery, and so would regard it not a piece of architecture at all. He comes very close to saying precisely that when he says that it could easily be mistaken for a brick kiln.

Jefferson's criticisms of his own efforts to build according to Palladian principles are also revelatory of still another aspect of his conception of good architecture. He in fact confesses that

> My essay in architecture has been so much subordinated to the laws of convenience, and affected also by the circumstance of change in the original design that it is liable to some unfavorable and just criticisms.[22]

Of course when Jefferson speaks of "convenience" in this context he usually has in mind certain practical departures from strict Palladian rules. Inside the house they included alcove beds, glass doors which open in tandem, and octagonal rooms which were not inspired by Palladio, but by plates in Robert Morris' *Select Architecture*. They allow, he thought, better window placement and better lighting.[23] On the outside Jefferson installed service

---

20   *TJ to Dr. John P. Emmet*, May 2, 1826. *L & B*, XVI, 171.
21   Cf. Richard R. Beeman, *Patrick Henry, A Biography*, 64; also Fawn M. Brodie, *Thomas Jefferson, An Intimate History*, 121-22.
22   *TJ to Benjamin Latrobe*, Oct. 10, 1809.
23   McLaughlin, 56, 61, 254-5.

wings beneath flat-roofed terrace walks in what Adams calls a "radical reversal of the Anglo-Palladian convention of a court-of-honor between extended wings,"[24] which had the disadvantage of blocking the surrounding view. Jefferson time and again allowed "the law of convenience" to supersede strict Palladian rules, and for these transgressions he was apologetic.[25] However, some architects and art historians have viewed these departures from Palladio for reasons of convenience and/or function as innovative improvements. Adams quotes Fiske Kimball[26] as saying that the "academic correctness and superior conveniences of Monticello" makes Jefferson a genuine "revivalist," and "the most Roman of the Romans."[27]

In 1799 the landscapist, Uvedale Price, published a book he entitled *The Picturesque,* and sent a copy to George Washington, who was apparently neither acquainted with the gardening trend nor with the term "picturesque." He found the subject "curious" and hoped to read the book when he found some leisure time.[28] In fact, Mount Vernon has some advantages over Monticello as far as picturesqueness is concerned. Being situated on a hill near the Potomac River, it has a spectacular vista whereas Monticello, although having a 360 degree view of forests and mountains, lacks the prospect of any such large body of water. Jefferson's friend, the Duc de la Rochefoucauld-Liancourt, who visited Monticello in 1796, found the ratio

> between the cultivated lands and those which are still covered with forests as ancient as the globe, at present much too great. The eye longs 'to discover' a broad river, a great

---

24 W, H. Adams, 63.

25 Jefferson once advised his friend Isaac Coles to obtain a copy of Palladio's *Four Books* and to "stick close to it." *Isaac Coles to John Harwell Cocke,* Feb. 23, 1816, but of course Jefferson himself had trouble doing so.

26 Fiske Kimball published all of Jefferson's architectural drawings in his book, *Thomas Jefferson Architect.* He thereby effectively silenced all those who attempted to deny that Jefferson was solely responsible for the design of the second phase of Monticello, the Capitol building in Richmond, and the entire design for the University of Virginia. It also silenced the allegation that the classical revival in America was started, not by Jefferson, but by Benjamin H. Latrobe. Cf. W. H. Adams, 240-41.

27 W.H. Adams, 82.

28 William M. S. Rasmussen & Robert S. Tilton, *George Washington: The Man Behind the Myths,* 184.

mass of water—destitute of which, the grandest and most extensive prospect is ever destitute of an embellishment requisite to render it completely beautiful.[29]

Jefferson himself was well aware of the aesthetic as well as the practical difficulties of building on a mountain-top. He said, "The grounds I destine to improve in the style of the English gardens are in a form very difficult to be managed."[30] He confesses in the same letter that to make it into an acceptable composition "would require much more of the genius of the landscape painter & gardener than I pretend to."

Other later criticisms of Monticello, based on the theory that art has meaning and that architecture, more perhaps than any other form of art, is essentially symbolic or metaphorical in character,[31] are perhaps not ones which Jefferson himself would accept. Consider, for example, the claim by such persons as Gaston Bachelard, Erik Ericson, and Jack McLaughlin that Jefferson's preference for octagonal and semi-octagonal rooms, as well as his selection of a dome for the second version of Monticello, reflect Jefferson's attempt to recapture maternal love and protection.[32] According to McLaughlin, "When Jefferson added the semi-octagons go his house, changing its geometry from angles to angled curves, he may at some very deep level have seen in this new form the suggestion of the house as bosom." The dome construction was an "obviously mammillary form."[33] On the other hand, it could be said, paraphrasing Freud regarding cigars, that sometimes an octagon is just an octagon, and a dome is just a dome.

A similar kind of "meaning" has been derived from the house's most glaring fault—its two stairways. An early visitor to Monticello, Mrs. William Thornton, complained that she "had to mount a little ladder of a

---

29   W.H. Adams, 158.

30   *TJ to William Hamilton,* July, 1806. Peterson, 1167; W. H. Adams, 170.

31   See Suzanne H. Crowhurst Lennard, *Explorations in the Meanings of Architecture*; also by the same author, "A House is a Metaphor," *Journal of Architectural Education,* XXVII, No. 2, 3, June, 1974.

32   McLaughlin, 62, who quotes Bachelard and Ericson to the same point.

33   Ibid.

staircase about two feet wide, and very steep."[34] Others have been similarly critical and have even hinted at misogyny on the part of Jefferson.

Of course it could be pointed out that octagonal rooms have certain architectural advantages over square or rectangular ones. The windows can be placed at better angles, eliminating dark corners, and generally adding light to the rooms. Domes also are advantageous in many respects. A single skylight can illuminate an entire room and repel rain and snow more efficiently than ordinary roofs. And as for the narrow staircases, it could be argued, as Jefferson himself argued, that they eliminate the grand "monarchical" or "royal" staircases which are expensive to build and occupy space on every story which could otherwise be used for additional rooms.

Some critics have attempted to attribute a kind of political meaning to Monticello. W. H. Adams says that "From the beginning, Jefferson envisioned the landscape around Monticello integrated into agricultural and food production as a thriving embodiment of his political idea of the agrarian state."[35] And again, "he strove to build a house harmonious with human dignity, the same ideal he followed in formulating the philosophy of the government."[36] The same sort of political meaning has been ascribed to Mount Vernon. The author who sent Washington a copy of his book, *The Picturesque*, according to William Rasmussen and Robert Tilton, "saw himself as liberating the landscape from unnatural tyranny" in much the same way that Washington had freed the nation."[37] Obviously he also wanted to incorporate the same sentiment, perhaps more explicitly, into Mount Vernon itself.

But as far as Jefferson is concerned, it is much more reasonable to take him at his word. His main concern as he told Madison was whether the Virginia Legislature would adopt his proposal to use the *Maison Carré* at Nîsmes, France, "this precious morsel of architecture left us by the antique world," as a model for the new State House in Richmond. He wanted to upgrade public architecture in America, as he said many times, and in this

---

34 Ibid., 5.
35 Adams, 157.
36 Ibid., ix.
37 Rasmussen and Tilton, 185.

case he thought that this building with which he had fallen in love[38] would help in that educative process. This was the basis of his enthusiasm for architectural art, not some thought of independence.

By his criticisms of the art and architecture of his day Jefferson reveals many of the aspects of a pragmatic theory of art. First, that the *raison d'etre* of art lies in its functionality, secondly, that it be environmentally friendly; thirdly, that it be rule-governed but not so tightly tied to principles that convenience is sacrificed. Pragmatists always look to the future and are willing to take risks and deviations from the conventional to achieve hoped-for beneficial consequences.

William James is another pragmatic thinker who emphasizes the central importance of the notion of functionality, but also of action or activity in art. He too cites certain psychologically based aesthetic principles which are far different from Jefferson's mathematically based Palladian rules, but not necessarily inconsistent with them.

WJ and his brother, Henry, the novelist, were in certain respects very much influenced in their views of art, both positively and negatively, by their father, Henry James, Senior, who held a rather peculiar but very definite view of art, in all its forms, and also of professional artists such as painters, sculptors, writers, presumably architects as well, and their artistic careers. According to Henry Senior, they all tend to create their works and then try to sell them for profit, an act which he personally regarded as anathema. As he summarized it,

> It is melancholy to see the crawling thing which society christens Art, and feeds into fawning sycophancy. [Art should be] the gush of God's life into every form of spontaneous speech and act. [It has been reduced to the mere] trick of a good eye, or a good hand.[39]

---

38   See *TJ to Madame La Contesse de Tesse,* Mar. 20, 1787, Peterson, 891. Writing to a cousin of Lafayette from Nîsmes, he reports: "Here I am, Madam, gazing whole hours at the Maison Quarree, like a lover at his mistress, . ."

39   F. O. Matthiessen. *The James Family,* 93.

Aside from his dislike of *trompe l'oeil* painting or good copiers or imitators, Henry Sr.'s main objection was that artists were turning art into a business. One can perhaps be permitted to speculate that he could espouse such a view because he was "pensioned for life" because of his own father's business success. It didn't bother him a bit that his own writings were ill-received and profitless. He wholeheartedly believed in art for art's sake alone. But of course no pragmatist could accept such a view of art as essentially useless,[40] and neither of his eldest sons did. Henry Jr. of course went on to make his living by selling his books. William, though he studied painting for a time, eventually gave it up and never attempted to paint again, not even as a pastime. His rationale seems to have been given in a letter to a friend written several years before he embarked on his attempt to gain an artistic education.

> In a year or two I shall know definitely whether I am suited to it or not. If not, it will be easy to withdraw. There is nothing on earth more deplorable than a bad artist.[41]

Like his father, William seemed to think that being a second–rate artist was totally unacceptable. Later in his *Principles of Psychology,* vol. II, 53, in a footnote, he evaluated his own artistic abilities as follows:

> I am myself a good draughtsman, and have a very lively interest in pictures, statues, *architecture,* and decoration, and a keen sensibility to artistic effects. But I am an extremely poor visualizer, and find myself often unable to reproduce in my mind's eye pictures I have most carefully examined. [Italics mine]

---

40 In James' *Psychology: The Briefer Course.* published two years after his two volume *The Principles of Psychology,* he comments that "The study of the harmful[in mental life] has been made the subject of a special branch called 'Psychiatry'—the science of insanity—and the study of the useless is made over to 'Aesthetics.' Aesthetics and Psychiatry will receive no special notice in this book." cf. xxviii.

41 Ibid., 95.

Although having given up art as a career, William retained a strong interest in art and seems to have visited all the museums in Europe to view the masterpieces. He recounts that once while visiting a museum in Venice he observed an English couple sitting in a cold room in February for more than an hour before Titian's painting "Assumption." He himself was anxious to leave for the sunshine outside, but before he left he couldn't help eavesdropping on their deliciously sentimental comments which he reported as follows: "Their honest hearts had been kept warm all the time by a glow of spurious sentiment that would have fairly made old Titian sick."[42] His father would no doubt have agreed with him in that judgment.

He did make one more or less final attempt to write a piece in the general field of aesthetics, a review of a German novel by Herman Grimm, a copy of which he sent to his brother who saw that it was published in the *Nation*. William, however, describes his effort as follows:

> . . . after sweating fearfully for three days, erasing, tearing my hair, copying, recopying, etc., etc., I have succeeded in finishing the enclosed. . . I feel that a living is hardly worth being gained at this price. Style is not my forte, and to strike the mean between pomposity and vulgar familiarity is indeed difficult.[43]

He comments in response to Henry's encouragement that "I really have no respect for this unprincipled literary wash that floods the world and don't see why I should be guilty of augmenting it." These passages show a marked similarity to the views of art and artists which his father expressed, although later on, in 1869, Henry Sr. is quoted by William James himself as saying "Henry has decidedly got a gift."

Perhaps encouraged by HJ's kind and appreciative remarks about his first effort at aesthetic criticism, WJ through correspondence

---

42 James, *Principles of Psychology*, II, 471-72.
43 This and the next several quotes are from Matthiessen, *The James Family*, 316-342. An attempt to correlate the actual correspondence between the brothers is difficult since Matthiessen rarely cites specific dates of the communications.

undertook an analysis of several of his brother's stories, notably, "The Story of a Masterpiece," "The Romance of Certain Old Clothes," "Poor Richard," and "A Most Extraordinary Case." His criticism of these earlier works are more or less indicative of his later criticism of HJ's novels. Although WJ found in them "a certain neatness and airy grace of touch, and a suppleness and freedom of movement," he objects to the male versus female subject matter in many of his stories and that there is "something cold about it" and shows "a want of heartiness or unction." To compensate for the lack of heartiness, in WJ's opinion, a story must have either "rare picturesque elements of some sort" or "much action." Apparently by being concerned "only with elements of everyday life," HJ's stories lacked both picturesqueness and action. What WJ really expected in particular was some exhibition of *moral* action. As he put it in comparison with the thoroughness of Balzac, "In yours the moral action was very lightly touched, and rather indicated than exhibited."

At some point in WJ's criticisms of his brother's literary output he seems to have thought that his efforts to reform HJ were futile. "The method seems perverse. 'Say it *out*, for God's sake,' they [his readers] cry, 'and be done with it.'" (JF, 341). "What shall I say of a book constructed on a method which so belies everything that *I* acknowledge as law? You've reversed every traditional canon of story telling (especially the fundamental one of *telling* the story, which you carefully avoid) and have created a new *genre littéraire* which I can't help thinking perverse . . ."

Perhaps enough has been said about WJ's ventures into aesthetic criticism of literature to suggest how he would deal in pragmatic fashion with public art had he chosen to discuss it. We can detect many of the principles by which pragmatists judge art, namely, the centrality of function, the emphasis placed on action ('pragma" after all in Greek means "action'), the end goal of utility or usefulness, and rule-governedness. All of these features we discovered in Jefferson's pragmatic approach to architecture, and it would seem that they also are to be found in James' views of the subject.

Some of his biographers have been dumbfounded that he didn't write a separate treatise on the principles of aesthetics.[44] However, there are in fact numerous references to the topic in his *Principles of Psychology,* so much so that at the end of his chapter on "Reasoning" he comments that "I may appear to have strayed from psychological analysis into aesthetic criticism." (371) And in another long chapter on "Necessary Truths and the Effects of Experience," he devotes a short section to "Aesthetic and Moral Principles." (672-75). Strewn throughout the book are numerous references to art and aesthetic principles, without, somewhat surprisingly, ever mentioning his brother's literary productions or his own aesthetic criticisms of them.

It may be appropriate here to note that Henry also did not write a separate treatise on aesthetic principles. In his case that fact may be explained by what Socrates, himself a stone-cutter,[45] discovered when he interrogated the artists of his day about the nature of art. He found that although they did indeed know how to produce their art, they were unable to give a coherent account of its character.[46] Or compare what WJ said about Shakespeare: "Why . . . does the death of Othello so stir the spectator's blood and leave him with a sense of reconcilement? Shakespeare himself could very likely not say why; for his invention, though rational, was not ratiocinative." (PP-II, 362). Or again, "If you ask your most educated friend why he prefers Titian to Paul Veronese, you will hardly get more of a reply; and you will probably get absolutely none if you inquire why Beethoven reminds him of Michael Angelo, . . His thought obeys a *nexus,* but cannot name it. And so it is with all those judgments of *experts* . . . (PP-II, 365). Even today if an artist is asked to explain his art, he or she will most likely tell the inquisitor to "look," "see," "feel," or "listen." It takes a philosopher, or at least a theoretically-minded person, to answer questions about the nature of art, and unfortunately, Henry was no philosopher.

It should not be so surprising that WJ wrote as much about aesthetics as he did, although mostly interstitially. His own studies of art have

---

44   See Gerald Myer's discussion, *William James: His Life and Thought,* 415-422.

45   Socrates' father was a stone-cutter and sculptor who is said to have cut stone for the Parthenon, and presumably taught his son the art and trade while doing so, which was the custom.

46   Cf. Plato, *Apology of Socrates,* 22, a-e.

already been noted, but many of his psychological theories, as we shall see, were based on or correlated with aesthetic considerations, and he was much concerned, as his writings on ethics indicate—one might say even obsessed by the relation between aesthetic and moral and metaphysical principles.

James is aware in his *Principles of Psychology* that "An adequate treatment of the way we come by our aesthetic and moral judgments would require a separate chapter," which he says, "I cannot conveniently include in this book." (PP-II, 675). Still it is somewhat amazing how much of his thinking about aesthetics is included in the book, albeit, in bits and pieces, and in his other writings. Although he could totally abandon art as a profession, obviously he could not get it altogether out of his head. For example, he states quite unhesitatingly that "The aesthetic principles are at bottom such *axioms* as that a note sounds good with its third and fifth, or that potatoes need salt." (PP-II, 672, italics mine). He follows that comment with a distinction between aesthetic principles which are *postulates*, but not *propositions* with regard to the real outside world. (PP-II, 677).

His use of *axioms* in this context merely refers to aesthetic judgments which are on a par with certain moral judgments such as "Murder is wrong" and "Gratitude for the receipt of kindness is appropriate behavior." These kinds of statements are assumed by civilized persons to be true, but are basically unexplained and await some justification by some larger principle or belief.

According to James, Nature exhibits two orders of things, a mechanical order and a sentimental order. The truths or general principles of science and mathematics are most compatible with and applicable to the "mechanical" order of things and as of now less rationally connected to the "sentimental"[47] order. General aesthetic principles for the most part apply only to relations between *entia rationis,* or terms of the mind. (PP-II, 677), in other words to the sentimental order. These he calls *postulates* with respect to the outer world because they are not factually true *propositions*. Thus, according to James, when we discuss aesthetics we are referring to

---

47 James is not here referring to the emotion of sentimentality which he finds totally objectionable in matters of art. Cf. his reaction (above, 33) to the English couple whose sentiments would have made Titian sick!

relations which exist in our minds, but do not "translate" into the objective world. As a result, one person's opinion of a piece of art may differ from that of another without contradiction, which would be the case if aesthetic judgments were empirical claims.

Their origin is "brain-born" or as he also says, "house-born" (PP-II, 627, 641). James disagrees with most British empiricists such as Hume, Mill, and Spencer who claim that all knowledge, all rationality, is derived from sense experience. James believes that much that is rational in character is the product of certain innate structures or "lines" in the mind, all however having physiological roots in the brain.

There are, however, basically two kinds of reasoning. One kind involves the isolation of a third term through which the premise is related to the conclusion; the other kind does not require the mediation of a "third term," but is of the nature of immediate inference, or more specifically is reasoning either by means of perceived "contiguity" or reasoning by means of "similarity." (PP-II, 325). Thus James distinguishes abstract reasoners, who reason mediationally and those whose reasoning is of a more spontaneous type and more in the nature of immediate inference. The first he calls "men of science, and philosophers—analysts, in a word" (PP-II, 361), and the second, persons such as "the poets, the critics,[48] the artists, in a word, the men of intuition."

James is fully aware of the importance of the artistic or intuitive temperament. In his article, "The Sentiment of Rationality," he fully develops the notion that many of our ethical and metaphysical beliefs are founded on basic, or primitive, preferences or intuitions, rather than on, as Kant would have it, "pure reason." In the *Principles* he summarizes some of those same thoughts as follows:

> Many of the so-called metaphysical principles are at bottom only expressions of aesthetic feeling. Nature is simply and invariable; makes no leaps, or makes nothing but leaps;

48 WJ may have inadvertently included critics here since he treats them later on as akin to philosophers and scientists.

is rationally intelligible; neither increases nor diminishes in quantity; flows from one principle, etc., etc.,—what do all such principles express save our sense of how pleasantly our intellect would feel if it had a Nature of that sort to deal with? (PP-II, 672).

And regarding moral principles he similarly maintains that

The most characteristically and peculiarly moral judgments that a man is ever called on to make are in unprecedented cases and lonely emergencies, where no popular rhetorical maxim can avail, and the hidden oracle alone can speak. (Ibid.).

From an art critic's point of view, however, certain general aesthetic principles must come into play. Aside from his references to an "order of taste," "canons of story telling," and "laws regarding writing methods," which, unfortunately, in his critiques of HJ's works he never fully elaborates, he does discuss at length in his *Principles of Psychology*, sometimes in whole chapters, many psychological principles which have aesthetic bearings, and which an intelligent critic probably should be intimately aware of. These include the Principle of Habit, which he admits cannot account for all aesthetic judgments, the Principles of Discrimination and Comparison, the Principle of Selection and Abstraction, and the Principle (or Law) of Association.

In his critiques of HJ's literary productions WJ pleads with him to write a book with no "twilight in the plot," no "fencing in the dialogue," no "psychological commentaries," but with "great vigor and decisiveness in the action," and "absolute straightness" in the style. If one were to imagine how WJ might similarly criticize the contemporary public art of Christo, Richard Serra, and John Seward Johnson, Jr., in terms of the pragmatic and psychological principles he enunciates, how might it go? With respect to Christo, he might object to the lack of utility in his productions. Since they are totally useless and regarded as "art for art's sake" alone, he might treat them strictly as **non-art,** much as Jefferson treated the Williamsburg Lunatic Asylum. In the case of Serra's site-specific and site-sensitive art, he might cite a certain contempt for human action and habits of behavior, or a minimal appreciation of functionality. So like Jefferson's evaluation of the Capitol Building in Williamsburg, he might assess it as less than perfectly right or beautiful art, but nonetheless having a **lower degree of art**. Regarding Johnson's "Forever Marilyn" sculpture, one can easily imagine his viewing it as a spurious attempt to provide a kind of pleasure or satisfaction, and ultimately failing to achieve that utilitarian consequence, and so a case of definitely "unchaste" or **bad art**.

On the other hand, like Jefferson who apologized for his departures from Palladian rules for reasons of convenience, WJ might also confess that he was only expressing his own intuitive preferences, or as he also calls them "ideals," which seemed to him the reverse of HJ's allegedly perverse methodology. He does in fact admit that "My taste is rather incompetent in these matters."[49] and furthermore, as the adage goes, *De gustibus non est disputandum.* Yet, later architectural historians and critics have generally approved of TJ's architectural innovations, despite his violation of Palladian rules. So also some may agree with WJ's rather severe treatment of his brother's literary style, and even regard as correct our application of his aesthetic principles to the more recent public art of Christo, Serra, and Johnson. The "de gustibus" principle may not apply here. In any case, WJ's decades-long persistence in criticizing his brother's works suggests that he did not really believe it true.

---

49 See F. O. Matthiessen, *The James Family.* 315-345, exact reference not found, but see corroborating reference, 340 (WJ to HJ, Feb. 1, 1906); also *The Correspondence of William James,* vol. III., 306.

Chapter III

SHOULD PUBLIC ART BE SUBSIDIZED? THE STATUE OF LIBERTY, THE GOLDEN GATE BRIDGE, AND NAZI ARCHITECTURE AS CASES IN POINT

It seems only right and proper that art which is directed at the People (i.e., Public Art) should be subsidized, if necessary for its creation, by the government of the People. We shall discover, however, that legislative bodies often refuse to provide such subsidies, and leave that task to the generosity of the private sector. Sometimes private donations are sufficient to meet the need, and sometimes not. Because such private subsidies often have "strings" or special conditions attached to them which can prejudice the art or make sycophants out of the artists, some critics have suggested that absolutely no subsidies be given either for public art, or for that matter, for any art. Since the financing of non-public art raises special difficulties which perhaps may not apply to public art, and public art subsidies may have difficulties which don't apply to non-public art, e.g., taxing the public for symphony orchestras which are heard only by a small number of persons, or museums which are generally unvisited, we shall restrict our attention in what follows to public art subsidies, and not to art subsidies generally.

In 1882, as a contribution to an auction of art and manuscripts to help finance the building of a pedestal for the Statue of Liberty, a gift from the People of France to the People of the United States of America, Emma Lazarus was asked to submit an original poem. At first she declined because she did not write poems for statues, but subsequently changed her mind apparently when she perceived a connection, over and above the international bond of friendship between France and America, between freedom in this country and the "golden door" of democracy.

She had at this time been very active in helping refugees from eastern Europe, particularly Russia, where anti-Semitic pogroms were taking place. As a result of this insight she submitted the famous sonnet now ensconced on a plaque in the Statue of Liberty Museum on Bedloe ('Liberty') Island in New York Harbor.

> "Give me your tired, your poor,
> Your huddled masses yearning to breathe free,
> The wretched refuse of your teeming shore.
> Send these, the homeless, tempest-tost to me,
> I lift my lamp beside the golden door!"

Opposite the "Golden Door" of the Statue of Liberty, on the western shore of the United States, is the "Golden Gate Bridge" of San Francisco Bay. It has been declared one of the "Wonders of the World" by the American Society of Engineers, which is probably an exaggeration since many such suspension bridges have been constructed which are much longer and higher, but it has also been acclaimed the "most beautiful" and the "most photographed" bridge in the world. The latter description is probably correct, but the former aesthetic judgment may still be debatable. In any case, its history tells us how difficult it has been in this country to get citizens to accept and finance public art, until its pragmatically beneficial consequences can be ascertained and vouched for.

The difficulties of financing the Golden Gate Bridge were not unlike the difficulties faced by those who sought to fund the Statue of Liberty. The sculpting of the statue by Frédéric Auguste Bartholdi, its transportation to the United States, and its assembly was meant to be a gift from the

People of France in celebration of American Independence,[1] and paid for by French donors. But the land on which it was to be erected and the pedestal on which it rests was to be funded by Americans. Because of the economic situation at the time, both countries had difficulties coming up with the money to pay for the project, the Americans more so than the French. Bedloe's Island was selected by General William T. Sherman of Civil War fame who was appointed to choose the site of the Statue of Liberty National Monument, to be administered first by the U.S. Lighthouse Board, then the Department of War, and finally by the National Park Service. No specific funds were required for this act. Congress, however, refused to appropriate funds for the pedestal and a resort to private funding had to be made.

Joseph Pulitzer, publisher of *The World* newspaper, was so astounded by the lack of donations that he undertook the project on his own, and in his editorials proceeded to prod and cajole wealthy citizens who had failed to come forth with contributions and also average citizens who seemed content to let the rich pay for it. In 1885 the economy was in a critical state, but finally Pulitzer's nagging paid off and sufficient funds wee obtained.

Financing the Golden Gate Bridge was similarly difficult. By an Act of the California Legislature in 1928, the Golden Gate Bridge and Highway District was formed and authorized to design, construct, and finance the project. After the Wall Street crash in 1929 private donations became unavailable, the Legislature appropriated none for the purpose, and so the District lobbied for and got approval for a $30 million bond measure. Even so there were no buyers and they were unable to sell the bonds until 1932 when Amadeo Giannini, founder of the Bank of Italy, which later merged with the Bank of America, bought the entire issue, and work then proceeded, starting in 1933 and ending in 1937, at a cost of over $35 million.

As a kind of footnote, it should be added that in the case of the Statue of Liberty, when the Statue required extensive restoration in 1982, Lee Iacocca, former Board President of Ford and later CEO of Chrysler, was appointed to head a fundraising program. The restoration was estimated

---

1 July 4, 1776 is inscribed on the tablet which the sculpted figure holds.

to cost $87 million. It was an overwhelming success; contributions flowed in to finance the restoration of both the Statue of Liberty and Ellis Island. By that time thousands of immigrants (including Iacocca's own relatives) had passed through New York Harbor viewing the Statue along the way and been processed at Ellis Island. They and their descendants by the tens of thousands were anxious to give back to the country some of what they had received.

Despite the obvious advantages of having a bridge spanning the San Francisco Bay from the City to the County of Marin to the north, there were many serious objections to building it, some of which are still relevant considerations. Before its construction, transportation from one point to the other had to be made by ferry boats, which was time consuming and inconvenient if hauling large or heavy items. Fortunately in this time period (1920's and 1930's) there were relatively few automobiles, but the new automobile industry in Detroit was anxious to increase the demand for automobiles, and they thought a bridge might do just that.

Many persons doubted that a bridge could be built across 4200 feet, the longest span, and there was the danger that because of earthquakes or unusually high winds it would collapse. The Department of War (as the Department of Defense was then known) was concerned that the bridge might interfere with ship traffic. The U. S. Navy had concerns about its causing ship collisions blocking access to one of the Navy's main ports. The Southern Pacific Railroad opposed the bridge because it ran a fleet of ferry boats and feared competition. It filed a lawsuit to prevent the bridge from being built. However, the bridge finally received the endorsements of the local governments, and construction began in 1933.

The designers of the bridge were multiple as in the case of the Statue of Liberty. The statue was basically sculpted by Frédéric Bertholdi, but the interior structure was designed by Alexandre Gustave Eiffel (of Eiffel Tower fame), and the whole project inspired by Edouard René de Laboulaye, a French law professor and politician. The designers of the Golden Gate Bridge were Joseph Strauss, Irving Morrow, Leon Mosseiff, and Charles Alton Ellis, all bridge engineers, but inspired by a young engineering student's design developed as far back as 1916. Now almost forgotten, his name was James Wilkins.

Morrow designed the shape of the towers and the Art Deco features on the towers, the lighting, the railings and walkways. The Bridge also has its poet (or "poetic admirer" just as the Statue of Liberty has Emma Lazarus. The chief engineer, Joseph Strauss, who later falsely claimed that the design of the bridge was all his, wrote a poem entitled, "The Mighty Task is Done" which is now attached to the Bridge. It has seven stanzas, the first and fourth of which go as follows:

> At last the mighty task is done;
> Resplendent in the western sun
> The Bridge looms mountain high;
> Its titan piers grip the ocean floor,
> Its towers pierce the sky.
> Launched midst a thousand hopes and fears,
> Damned by a thousand hostile sneers,
> Yet ne'er its course was stayed,
> But ask of those who met the foe
> Who stood alone when faith was low,
> Ask them the price they paid.

About the time the Golden Gate Bridge was being constructed (1932-1937) in California, the Nazi Party in Germany was coming into power and introducing, along with their fascist regime, a wholly different conception of art and architecture. Hitler had been since his youth a great admirer of Roman civilization and the architecture for which they are known, such as the Coliseum in Rome (no doubt in part because of the vicious gladiator games performed there) and other grandiose structures traceable back to buildings such as the Parthenon located atop the Acropolis in Athens, and ancient Greek culture. In his imagination he held the idea that Greece was the primary descendant of an ancient Aryan culture from which the race of Germans was spawned. He considered it his duty to "weed out" the non-Aryan peoples (mostly Jews and Blacks) from Germany and eugenically to "purify" the race. He would prove to the world that Germans were superior to all other peoples. For some such reason he was eager to have the Olympic Games of 1936 held in Germany, and had a vision that all future games would be held there. What a disappointment it must have been to him when a black American, Jesse Owens, won the gold in track!

He hated what he called "degenerate art," and indeed all art and architecture which he thought did not serve or reflect the interests of the State. In 1937 the Nazis staged an exhibit of some 5000 works of confiscated art, some of it by such artists as Marc Chagall, Henri Matisse, Paul Klee, Pablo Picasso, and Vincent van Gogh. In 1942, at night in the gardens of the Galerie Nationale de Jeu de Paume, in Paris, many other such art works were destroyed in a bonfire. And as everyone knows, toward to end of the war the Nazis tried to export all the French art they could get their hands on back to Germany, but failing in that task tried to destroy it in accordance with Hitler's end of war "scorched earth" policy. Much of that art, some of it "degenerate" by their standards, was retrieved by U.S. forces and returned to France. Much was also siphoned off by the Russians and taken to the Hermitage in St. Petersburg, where it may still reside.

Hitler was especially critical of art thought to demean religion; sculptures and paintings by Jews; depictions he thought were insulting to womanhood, soldiers of the Third Reich, or German farmers; scenes reflecting insane or sick minds, or depraved views of Nature. Styles the Nazis regarded as degenerate included Bauhaus architecture; modernism, cubism, impressionism, and surrealism in painting. In sculpture, he favored neo-classical works, especially the work of German sculptor, Arno Breker, whose works were all in that conservative style. In fact Hitler made Breker the official state sculptor the very year (1937) Breker joined the Nazi Party. Besides monumental sculptures such as one representing a decathlete ("Der Zehnkämpfer") and another called The Victress ("Die Siegerin") for the 1936 Olympic Games, he produced a multiplicity of bronze "portraits."

His depictions in stone of the nude male body led Aristide Maillol to dub him "Germany's Michelangelo."[2]

Albert Speer (1905-1981) after studying architecture at several technical Universities in Germany, and becoming an assistant to Heinrich Tessenow, a well known architect and professor, he sought to practice architecture on his own with little success. In 1931 commissions in Germany, as well as in the rest of the world, were difficult to obtain, and he settled for a job managing his father's properties. He became a member of the Nazi Party, and the Party Leader for the West End of Berlin hired him without any fee to decorate his villa. The recipient was so pleased with the result that he recommended him to Joseph Goebbels to renovate the Party's Berlin Headquarters, presumably for a fee this time. After that success and after the Nazis had taken control of the government, Speer was commissioned to design the 1933 May Day Commemoration in Berlin. He used giant flags, which his former professor Tessenow thought showy and generally disapproved, but which Hitler himself found absolutely delightful. From then on commissions and subsidies and honors from the Nazi Party flowed in. He was made Nazi Party Commissioner for the Artistic and Technical Presentation of Party Rallies and Demonstrations, and in 1934 became the Party's head architect. One of his biggest commissions was the building of the Zeppelinfeld Stadium, which became the Nuremburg parade grounds and setting for Party rallies. It could accommodate 340,000 people, and is where Hitler often gave his fiery and angry speeches. In this architectural venture, neo-classical in style, not only did Speer make the backdrop for the events monumentally large, he surrounded it with anti-aircraft sized searchlights creating what he called "a cathedral of light" for meetings held there at night. No wonder that Hitler made him the Reich's chief architect answerable only to him, and with virtual control over many other government departments.

In 1938 Hitler asked Speer to design and build a new Reich Chancellery which would dwarf the old one. He specified that he needed to have it

---

2 Cf. Wikipedia, entry, "Arno Breker."

completed within one year for a reception of diplomats to be held on Jan. 10, 1939. Speer accepted the task (and the commission) and completed the building two days short of the deadline, and fully furnished! He accomplished this by using forced slave labor provided by thousands of workers conscripted from occupied foreign countries. The building was constructed on monumental lines and contained a "Marble Gallery" which was 146 meters long and could easily have enclosed the entire Hall of Mirrors in the Palace of Versailles[3]. Primarily because of his use of slave labor, Speer was later sentenced by the Nuremburg Tribunal to 20 years in Spandau prison.[4] But immediately after its completion he received from Hitler himself the "Nazi Golden Party Badge."

What now can be said about Nazi art and architecture in general, and of the chief sculptors and architects who produced it? First, neither Hitler nor his architects created a particular style of architecture as easily recognized as, say, Soviet architecture, whose buildings all tend to resemble warehouses. Hitler was content with the neo-classical style of ancient Greece and Rome and sought only to magnify them to heighten the image of the Nazi State. So also Nazi sculptures, especially those of Arno Breker—nothing particularly original about them except their monstrous size. In his books, Speer mentions Hitler's megalomania, and admits that he tried to accommodate the Führer's extravagant notions about art and architecture.

What comes through loud and clear is the fact that both Speer and Breker, although extremely talented and well trained, were desperate for commissions when they started their careers. Although private sponsors were still in existence during Hitler's rise, they were relatively few, partly because of the world-wide depression at that time and because if the art

---

3 According to Speer, Hitler ordered a total reshaping of the city of Berlin with a north-south axis boulevard which was to have a triumphal arch, grander in size than the Arc de Triomphe on the Champs Élysée in Paris. It was never constructed.

4 Two Soviet judges and one American on the Nuremburg Court were in favor of the death penalty for Speer even though he was the only Nazi defendant who openly admitted that he had abdicated his moral responsibility in his support of Hitler, first as his chief architect and later as his very efficient Minister of Armaments and War Production. After serving every day of his twenty year sentence, he wrote two best selling books, *Inside the Third Reich* and *Spandau: The Secret Diaries;* and later a book entitled *Infiltration* about the SS.

or buildings produced did not meet Hitler's tastes or requirement, they were confiscated and destroyed. State sponsorship seemed to these talented individuals to be about the only way to survive professionally. But their acceptance of such subsidies, as we now know, only created much spectacular but on the whole pretentious art, and furthermore, made sycophants, as Henry James, Senior, would say, out of the artists who collaborated with Hitler and the Nazi regime.

We cannot, of course, condemn state subsidies for public art generally, for the Nazi case is only a very extreme example of what can happen, but it does point up the fact that dependence on the largess of government has its dubious and sometimes regrettable aspects.

Chapter IV

MUST PUBLIC ART ALWAYS BE FOR THE PEOPLE? DOES PRAGMATISM DICTATE DEMOCRACY?

In his *Gettysburg Address,* Abraham Lincoln extols "Government of the people, by the people, and for the people," suggests that it is mankind's "last best hope," [1] and expresses his sincere wish that "it shall not perish from the earth." Adolf Hitler in a comparable claim was somewhat less extravagant. He only hoped that his Third Reich, or some form of government derived from it, would "last a thousand years." Like all tyrants he despised democracy, or "government *of* and *by* the people," and substituted for it a government run only by Nazi Party members such as Albert Speer and Arno Breker. Yet it is fairly clear that he thought it should be, or would be if his schemes were enacted, a government *for* the people, even if by that expression he meant only to include the German People, or at least People of Aryan Ancestry.

The question, though, does arise, why should he be so adamantly opposed to democracy as an ideal political goal? Most historians probably would say that it had to do with Germany's defeat in WWI, his dissatisfaction with the subsequent Weimar Republic, and no doubt for other reasons given in his autobiographical account, *Mein Kampf.* What is so disturbing

---

1   These exact words, "last best hope," are in fact from his annual message to Congress, Dec.1, 1862.

about his position, however, to an advocate of pragmatic philosophy, is that many of his views, particularly as they pertain to art and architecture, bear a certain resemblance to those of acknowledged pragmatists such as William James, John Dewey, and Thomas Jefferson, none of whom would ever have subscribed to the political tenets which Hitler espouses.

For example, the *Autobahn* he had constructed throughout Germany, and other highways in Austria, such as the one leading to his "Eagle's Nest" residence near Berchtesgaden in the Alps above Salzburg (a most beautiful vista, by the way), were not meant simply as motorways, but to function symbolically as evidence of a united Germany, linking one part of the Fatherland to the others. Buildings adorned with the swastika were not only to be parts of the city or the landscape, but were built to direct traffic in and about them in accordance with the desires of the builder or architect to create certain attitudes favorable to the city or state. Unlike other arts, Hitler's architects and artisans realized that architecture has this capacity to stimulate and cause certain types of behavior or action. These concerns with action and function are clearly aspects of any pragmatic theory of art and architecture.

Although Nazi architecture was primarily based on the classical structures of Greece and Rome, they were intended to be focused on the future, not on what they conceived to be the decadent past, or on anything associated with the Weimar Republic. This futuristic emphasis is also characteristic of pragmatism. They thought that architecture should be useful, i.e., it should serve a utilitarian function, as pragmatists also demand, but again, like the pragmatists, such consequentialism need not focus exclusively on the production of pleasure.[2] William James makes it quite clear that although he agrees with consequentialism, he does not agree with the utilitarians that the ultimate moral goal is pleasure, even for the greatest number.[3] The grandiose architecture of the Nazis was on the contrary meant to be intimidating,

2 Cf. http://en. Wikipedia.org/wiki/Nazi Architecture
3 James, "The Moral Philosopher and the Moral Life," in *Essays on Faith and Morals,* 186; Holmes too questions why the good of the greatest number should be our primary goal. See "The Gas Stokers Strike," 7 ALR 582 (1873) reprinted in Lerner, 51.

powerful, and something to be feared. None of the pragmatists held such a view, but they did agree with the Nazis that the ultimate end or goal of art and architecture need not be simply a pleasant experience.[4] The Nazi even went much farther than we have suggested: they wanted to dominate the world, whether the conquered peoples liked it or not!

Hitler wanted his architecture to be friendly to the environment, and thought all negative depictions of Nature "degenerate." And just as Thomas Jefferson agreed with Francis Bacon's appreciation of the garden ("Without [gardens] buildings and palaces are but gross handiworks." cf. above 23-24), so Hitler appreciated Nature and natural settings, e.g., for his *autobahns, volkshalle,* and *Berchtesgaden* retreat.

Instead of the gloomy interiors of the great Cathedrals of Europe, he wanted his public buildings such as the *Volkshalle* ("Peoples' Halls") to be light and airy. One cannot help but compare his views regarding interior illumination with Jefferson's use of octagonal rooms and ceiling domes so as to maximize lighting. Although he had no use for religion as such or the Catholic Church in particular, he did admire one aspect of the dark and gloomy interiors of cathedrals. He observed that those artificially created gloomy environments made the religious practitioners more submissive to authority and less self-interested, and he desired to create those same effects in the audiences who attended his public meetings at the Zeppelinfeld Stadium and elsewhere.

Hitler also insisted that his architecture and his designs for roadways, towns, and cities be orderly and rule-governed. In *Mein Kampf* he complains that many German cities lacked a sense of national community, vigorous public monuments, and general orderliness. He once told the Mayor of Berlin that his city was "unsystematic." Hitler's opinion of Bauhaus architecture, with its leaner and, compared to neoclassicism, less decorated style, was similarly without rational order or design and so "degenerate." Although modern pragmatic architects may differ with Hitler regarding Bauhaus concepts, still most of them from Thomas Jefferson to Frank

---

4   We may later on in our discussion of John Dewey's views have to modify this claim somewhat.

Lloyd Wright have upheld the notion that architecture has to obey certain objective rules.

But perhaps enough has been said about the somewhat frightening similarity between Hitler's architectural notions and typically American notions of pragmatic architectural philosophy. Is there a crucial difference, and what is it? The main reason Nazism is not to be classed as a form of pragmatism is that the Nazis, unlike the pragmatists, are dogmatic about the ultimate moral and political goals of society. Nazis in this respect are more like Marxists and Utilitarians who, as pointed out in another context,[5] set pre-established or a priori goals. Marxists aim at a classless society; Utilitarians, the greatest happiness for the greatest number. Pragmatists deliberately and on principle resist setting such goals. As William James puts it: "[Pragmatism] does not stand for any special results. It is a method only . . . It appears less as a solution . . . than as a program for more work . . ."[6]

Richard Rorty, a self-proclaimed disciple of John Dewey, enlarges on this notion when he says, "When [Dewey] uses 'truly democratic' as a supreme honorific, he is obviously envisaging an achieved America. Both Dewey and [Walt] Whitman viewed the United States as an opportunity to see ultimate significance in a finite, human project . . . Democracy, Dewey said, 'is neither a form of government nor a social expediency, but a metaphysic of the relation of man and his experience in nature'"[7] Taking exception to Dewey's use of the word "metaphysic," Rorty thinks that Dewey "might have expressed his meaning better by saying that democracy is the principal means by which a more evolved form of humanity will come into existence."[8] But Rorty is generally in agreement with Dewey's view of the relation between American democracy and the human goals of freedom and equality, provided that it is understood that democracy is still an uncompleted experiment, something yet to be achieved.

---

5 Cf. Davis, *Comparative Philosophy: Four Philosophical Americans,* 80-81, 92, n.13, 104.
6 James, *Pragmatism: A New Name For Some Old Ways of Thinking,* 51, 53.
7 Rorty, *Achieving Our Country,* 17-18.
8 Ibid., 142, n.12.

Justice Oliver Wendell Holmes, another pragmatic thinker,[9] has put the point about as well as it can be put when he said in his dissenting opinion in *Gitlow v. N.Y.,* 268 U.S. 652 (1925), a case involving freedom of speech, that "If in the long run the beliefs expressed in proletarian dictatorship are destined to be accepted by the dominant forces of the community[10], the only meaning of free speech is that they should be given their chance and have their way." Although Holmes was in no way committed to a government based on a "proletarian dictatorship," still in a democracy in which free speech is valued, such radically different views should be allowed if found acceptable by the "dominant forces of the community," and incorporated, but not of course until their superior merits had been established, a view which is clearly consistent with what James called "pragmatic openness of mind."[11]

Despite their hesitancy in adopting in advance of actual experience any set of social values as the ultimate end of society, it is fairly obvious that James, Dewey, and Holmes, as well as Lincoln, all subscribe to the democratic notion of government of, by, and for the people. The question, however, is what is there in their pragmatic philosophies which justifies their belief? In upholding that belief are they being just as dogmatic as the Marxists, Utilitarians, and Nazis? To put the matter even more strongly, does pragmatism dictate, or in some fundamental way, imply democracy, or at least such values as freedom and equality without which democracy could not exist?

Negatively expressed, pragmatists do not see the world, nature, or reality, call it what you will, as "some divinely instituted world-enigma"[12] of which our ideas are but copies, nor is "mind as such . . . a mere mirror."[13]

---

9 A controversy still exists as to whether Holmes was a pragmatist, but see my argument that he definitely was. *Comparative Philosophy,* 82-3.

10 Jefferson held the same view regarding what he called the "living generation" or dominant majority. Cf. his letter to James Madison, Sept. 6, 1789, in Peterson, 959-64. Also, *First Inaugural Address,* 492-3, in Peterson, 492-493; Also Davis, *Comparative Philosophy,* 152, where it is described as his first prolegomenon.

11 James, see his *Dedication* of *Pragmatism* to John Stuart Mill.

12 James, *Pragmatism* and *The Meaning of Truth,* 94.

13 James, "An Interiew," quoted in H.S. Thayer, *Pragmatism: The Classical Writings,* 133.

More positively, pragmatists see the world as a "stream of experience" (James' expression, akin to his "stream of consciousness" notion, but also accepted by and elaborated upon by Dewey[14]) in which ideas are contiguous with objects and "our theories are instrumental mental modes of adaptation to reality."[15] A thought, according to the Peircean formula which all pragmatists accept in one form or another, means only "the conceivable effects of a practical kind an object may involve." Or as Holmes puts it, "All thought is social, on its way to action."[16]

Apply these notions to the Jeffersonian idea that "all men are created equal." If our ideas and theories were merely photocopies of reality, would we not have to say, because of the inequalities of men, that the ideal is a false one, and so not acceptable as a fundamental tenet of democracy? The pragmatist does not see it that way. The social and political idea of equality, and the same could be said for freedom, is only "on its way to action." According to James, like any fundamental idea,

> You must . . . set it at work within the stream of your experience. It appears . . . more particularly as an indication of the ways in which existing realities may be *changed* . . . Theories then become *instruments* . . . We don't lie back upon them, we move forward, and, on occasion, make nature over again by their aid.[17]

Rorty's insightful distinction between an "achieved" democracy or America and one that is only in the process of being achieved presupposes the same point, Whatever our democratic ideas are now, and freedom and equality are among them, they are in the process of being achieved. Thus pragmatism is "friendly" to democracy in the negative sense that it does not reject freedom and equality as pillars of democracy simply because in fact, at

---

14 James, *Pragmatism*, 32; Dewey, *Experience and Nature*, 232, 312-13.
15 James, *Pragmatism*, 94.
16 O. W. Holmes, Jr., "John Marshall," in Max Lerner, *The Mind and Faith of Justice Holmes*, 385
17 *Pragmatism*, 31-2.

present, not all men are equally free, as a representational realist (or copy theorist) would consistently have to do. But is it friendly in the more positive sense of implying democracy, as contrasted with, say, communism or fascism?

Philosophical pragmatism, as so far described, only provides a method for deciding between competitive theories which is the most beneficial or satisfactory in terms of their practical consequences. But if one takes seriously the views of Walt Whitman who literally identifies Democracy with America, or Mark Twain, whose writings exemplify American democracy at its best and at its worst,[18] or John Dewey who speaks of what is "truly democratic," it is pretty obvious that these thinkers among millions of others have concluded that, as a work in progress and as a way of life, and as a matter of fact, democracy has surpassed all other systems as far as long range benefits to mankind are concerned.

But consider also what happened when Hitler shut down the Bauhaus School of Art when he came to power in 1933. Germany lost one of the most progressive and influential group of artists and architects the world has ever seen. From 1919 to 1933 the Bauhaus School created an entirely new modernistic style which has been extremely influential around the world. What happened to the resident architects and founders, Walter Gropius and Ludwig Mies van de Rohe? Both exiled themselves to the United States, Gropius accepting a position at the Harvard University Graduate School of Design and Mies accepting a similar position in Chicago. Like other German and Austrian émigrés, such as Albert Einstein, Edward Teller, Max Born, Sigmund Freud, and others in the fields of physics, mathematics, and psychology, they chose to go to democratic countries such as England and the United States, where they were free to pursue their intellectual interests. A comment by Einstein is very revelatory of what they found in those countries.

---

18 According to Bernard De Voto in *Mark Twain's America* (1932), 321, "There is more America in Mark Twain's books than in any others." He calls Twain's views "centripetal Americanism" because he frequently was seen, and in some quarters still is seen, as the spokesman for the entire nation. *The Portable Mark Twain*, 29.

"What makes the new arrival devoted to this country is the democratic trait among the people. No one humbles himself before another person or class . . . American youth has the good fortune not to have its outlook troubled by outworn traditions."[19]

Naturally many of these emigrants were reluctant to leave their homelands, but were forced to because of the vicious policies of the Nazis who denied them their freedom and regarded the many Jews among them as unequal and "inferior." When the Nazi came to power in 1933 they burned all of Freud's books.[20] Although his life was in danger, he tried to stay in Austria as long as he could. It is interesting that Freud had to be persuaded by an English friend and fellow psychiatrist, Dr. Ernest Jones, to move to London where he was able to pursue his work unhindered until his death there in 1939.

There is still another way of looking at the relation between democracy and pragmatic theories of art and architecture. The term "architect" as used to describe someone like Thomas Jefferson, Frank Lloyd Wright, Walter Gropius, Ludwig Mies, or even Albert Speer, commonly means a person who designs buildings or in some cases whole cities. But there is a much larger and grander sense of the term which is intended when one speaks of Jefferson, for instance, as the "architect of the government of the United States," or an "architect of democracy." He was, after all, the chief writer of the Declaration of Independence, the author of hundreds of laws by which our government was first run, and served as our third President, during which time he tried his best to see that our Constitution was rigidly adhered to.[21]

---

19 Quoted in Walter Isaacson, *Einstein: His Life and Universe*, 407.

20 Freud is quoted as saying, "What progress we are making. In the Middle Ages they would have burned me. Now they are content with burning my books." Cf. Wikipedia, "Sigmund Freud."

21 Although Jefferson initiated the purchase of the Louisiana Territory from France, and thereby nearly doubled the size of the country, he himself had misgivings about his actions since nowhere in the Constitution was he given the power to do so. But no one seemed to care, with the possible exception of John Quincy Adams. See Dumas Malone, *Jefferson The President: First Term*, 330.

There are others who also deserve the appellation, "architect of our democracy," for example, Walt Whitman whom William James called "a contemporary prophet" who "felt the human crowd as rapturously as Wordsworth felt the mountains;"[22] and Mark Twain, whom Bernard De Voto thinks " helped to develop the modern American style," whose books are "the first American literature of the highest rank which portrays the ordinary bulk of Americans . . . and delineates their hopes, fears, decencies, and indecencies as from within," and who expresses his belief in democracy implicitly or explicitly in all his books.[23] John Dewey has also been an extremely influential "architect" with respect to American education and many other aspects of American Life. Add also, William James, whose "architectural" contributions to psychology and philosophy have had international effects; and Oliver Wendell Holmes, Jr, most famously known for his dissents on the U. S. Supreme Court, is acknowledged as the primary founder and "architect" of modern American jurisprudence. Typically all of these persons espouse a generally pragmatic perspective whatever their individual fields of specialization.[24]

Still another way of perceiving the relation between pragmatism and democracy is to look upon all of the aforementioned persons as "builders," which is often a term used instead of, or in addition to, the term "architect." Jefferson was in a very practical way the builder of his beloved Monticello, but he was also a builder of his new country. A book about him is quite appropriately called *Jefferson: a Builder.*[25] Nor would it be particularly strange to call Whitman, Twain, Dewey, James, and Holmes, and Lincoln builders in this particular sense of the term.

Another group of Americans have also been called "builders" but they must be distinguished from those just mentioned. A fairly recent television series produced by Lionsgate and presented on the History channel is officially called *The Men Who Built America*. It depicts the lives and

22 James, *Essays on Faith and Morals*, 272

23 Bernard De Voto, Introduction, *The Portable Mark Twain*,26.

24 For further confirmation of this contention see Davis, Comparative *Philosophy: Four Philosophical Americans*, 173.

25 See Jack McLaughlin, *Jefferson and Monticello: The Biography of a Builder* (Henry Holt, 1988).

accomplishments of several Barons of Industry, namely, Commodore Vanderbilt, John J. Rockefeller, Sr., Andrew Carnegie, J.P. Morgan, and Henry Ford. It is an extremely well made and intensely interesting documentary which, somewhat surprisingly, happens to be historically quite accurate. The publicity for the film reads "Meet the titans who forged the foundation of modern America and created the American Dream!" "America wasn't discovered. It was built."

Unlike Whitman, Twain, Dewey, and the others, as far as these Barons of Industry were concerned, "America" did not equate with "Democracy." Their actions belie any belief that they aimed at building a democratic country or a government of, by, and for the people. Their primary aim was the aggregation of wealth for themselves alone. Vanderbilt didn't acquire railroads and attempt to monopolize the industry in order to expand the country or create jobs for his countrymen, although that did occur as a by-product. Rockefeller didn't create the Standard Oil Company to produce and deliver kerosene and later gasoline in order to upgrade the living standards of the people, although that did happen as a largely unintended consequence. Nor did Carnegie manufacture steel to improve public bridges or create housing and offices in skyscraper buildings for city dwellers though those architectural accomplishments were achieved. Morgan did not cannibalize smaller industries and struggling companies to benefit the average stockholder. Even Edison, whom Morgan subsidized to bring about electric lighting in residences and city streets, became infected with a self-centered mercenary interest. So too was Henry Ford but to a lesser extent since he paid his workers a living wage and provided better working conditions in his factories; his democratic image suffered, however, because of his admitted anti-Semitism.

The documentary shows quite clearly how Carnegie engaged in a de-cades-long rivalry with Rockefeller, not regarding who could produce a better America, but who could amass the most dollars. When politicians such as William Jennings Bryan sought to control their rapaciousness by getting the legislatures and Congress to pass anti-trust laws, the Barons pooled as much of their wealth and power as was necessary to "buy" the next President, William McKinley, whom they thought would be more sympathetic to their pecuniary interests and leave them alone to gouge the public as they saw fit. It worked well until McKinley was assassinated and "Teddy" Roosevelt became president and managed to get such legislation passed.

The political and social goals of democracy—the good of the public—was never their goal. What they were "builders" or "architects" of was the Golden Calf of Wealth, not the Golden Door of Democracy, nor the Golden Gate of Freedom, but something more akin to Hitler's Golden Badge of Power.

It must be said as a postscript, however, that many of these Barons of Industry, who laid the groundwork for the materialistic and technological development of our country, after their retirements, sought to atone for their past behavior. Carnegie, for instance, presumably because of his partial responsibility for the Johnstown Flood (1889) in which some 2209 persons lost their lives, gave millions of dollars to communities throughout the land to build library buildings. He also donated a grand Music Hall in New City ("Carnegie Hall"). Henry Clay Frick, his one-time business partner and notorious labor manager donated his own personal art collection to a museum bearing his name also in New York City. Rockefeller money created a masterpiece of skyscraper construction known as Rockefeller Center, with several inner courts displaying public art statuary. His namesake, John D. Rockefeller, Jr. is responsible for the magnificent reconstruction of Historic Williamsburg in Virginia. Indeed, it has to be admitted that the offspring of many of these old Barons of Industry did what their ancestors did not, or did only belatedly. They were responsible for some of the best public (and non-public) art in the country.

Chapter V

WHY POLITICIZE ART? A DIVERSITY OF OPINION REGARDING THE FINAL CAUSES OF PUBLIC ART

There are many different reasons why public art is promoted, encouraged, sponsored, subsidized, and/or tolerated by certain individual patrons; governments, as diverse as democracies, dictatorships, and communisms; various mutually antagonistic religious sects including those of Islam, Judaism, and Christianity; and numerous business and other competitive economic groups. Their views do not always intermesh and are at times positively hostile to one another. The public art and architecture they encourage often sends out mixed, multiple, and sometimes belligerent messages. Let us attempt to sort out these views by means of an explanatory scheme worked out by Aristotle for understanding the "causes" of certain human acts, things, and events. It is called his Theory of the Four Causes.

Suppose, for example, we are trying to understand the rationale of an object such as a house (or bridge, statue, or whatever). According to Aristotle we should first ask about its "material cause," i.e., what it is made of. Next we need to know its "formal cause," the plan or design of the object. Third, it would be informative to know its "efficient cause," who designed or actually built it. Lastly in order to understand it fully, we need to know its "final cause," or what purpose or purposes it is supposed to serve.

Some persons in their evaluations of a piece of public art or architecture never get past asking about its material cause. Hitler, or at least Albert Speer, seems to have been that way about buildings constructed of concrete reinforced by re-bars, or built with steel girders. Speer's Theory of Ruin Value was that buildings should be built so that even after a thousand years the buildings in ruin would still give the viewer an idea of the grandeur they had had in Hitler's day. Reinforced concrete and steel girders tend over time to rust and decay leaving nothing behind. Hitler loved Speer's idea and didn't want any of his buildings constructed of those (very modern) materials.

Others judge a house primarily in terms of its "formal" cause. Bacon, for example, emphasized the importance of placing the building within a garden setting without which he said even palaces were but mere "handiworks."

Some judge buildings solely by their designer or architect. Building styles tend to reflect rather consistently their maker's mentality, such that a house designed by Frank Lloyd Wright is unmistakable even if only viewed casually, and for some persons, that is all one needs to know about the place. Many a person or corporation has commissioned Wright and has simply given Wright his head, sat back, and waited to see what he would produce for them.

Judging a house in terms of its "final" cause is considerably more complex, for people's ideas about what a house is for, its primary purpose, and how well a particular house fulfils that purpose differ widely.

Nothing seems more natural, when creating art for the People than to politicize it, that is, to give it a public meaning. Thus public statues and entire public buildings are often designed to suggest certain political ideals or goals. That intention was certainly the case with respect to the Statute of Liberty. Other public art celebrates heroism and patriotism. Think of the War Memorials around the world, and all the statues of Army Generals astride gallant steeds from George Washington to Robert E. Lee. Think also of all the structures built to honor our greatest presidents, Thomas Jefferson and Abraham Lincoln, as well other major contributors to democratic society here and around the world, persons such as Fiorello LaGuardia, Martin Luther King, Winston Churchill, and Nelson Mandela. We create statues and erect buildings to remind ourselves of their greatness, as we also do in other fields such as education, science, sports, medicine, law, and historically and most notably and extensively in religion with statuary and paintings dedicated to the Virgin Mary, Our Lady of Guadalupe, Jesus of Nazareth, Moses, Buddha, Shiva, and the like. As a matter of historical fact, however, none of these artistic endeavors which celebrate a society's values, or its appreciation of great achievement, is particularly new. The ancient Greeks and Romans, and before them many other tribes of peoples, did the same thing with their triumphal arches and religious temples. But herein we also witness conflict.

One nation's "triumph" is another's defeat, and one people's heroes are viewed by others as enemies or traitors. One man's god, or gods, is another's demon or demons. Even within the same religious framework, say, Islam or Christianity, there are many differences of opinion about ideals, goals, and "greatness." Jefferson once expressed his view that John Calvin's God was "a demon of malignant spirit" and that "it would be more pardonable to believe in no god at all, than to blaspheme him by the atrocious attributes of Calvin".[1] He would no more want a statue erected to honor Calvin than Hitler would want a statue of Abraham Lincoln erected at Berchtesgaden. Wars have been fought over such differences of opinion and much public art has been destroyed. Consider the precious and over 1500 year old giant carvings of two Buddhas on a cliff in Afghanistan (one 53 meters tall and the other 35 meters) which a Taliban mullah named Mohammed Omar ordered obliterated in March, 2001, because he thought them blasphemous and contrary to Sharia law. Despite protests and pleas from numerous countries around the world, including the United States, India, and Pakistan, he had the figures first shelled with artillery and then reduced to dust by dynamite. Consider also how statues of Saddem Hussein in Teheran were torn to the ground after he was

---

1 TJ to John Adams, April 11, 1823. Peterson, 1466.

captured and before he was executed. Statues of Mussolini in Italy were similarly destroyed after he was captured and shot to death. So angry were his fellow Italians that they hung his body upside down on meat hooks, stoned it, and spat upon it. Yet strangely many of the art works Mussolini is responsible for in Rome such as his grand boulevard, the Via dei Foro Imperiali still remain, as does his Foro Italico sports complex where the floors in mosaic tile read "Duce," "Duce," "Duce." Many of the Nazi structures created by Speer, such as the newly built Reich Chancellery have been destroyed, as has the Machzentium Palace for the Führer, the marble from which was taken by the Russians and used to erect a Soviet War Memorial in East Berlin.

Public art controversies and disagreements can be very complex and involved. For example, Mark Twain reports that while traveling and lecturing around the world, to mostly British colonial possessions, in an attempt to extricate himself from bankruptcy, he noticed in New Zealand a monument commemorating and naming a few (about 20) Maoris who in a fight for independence had chosen to fight with the British against their own people. Twain regarded the rebellious Maoris as the true patriots, and those who sided with their colonial rulers as traitors. His reaction to the monument: "Pull it down. It is a disgrace to both parties—traitors and those who praise them."[2]

In a similar vein he attacked other colonial powers of the time such as the Belgians for their mal-treatment of the natives of the Congo and the English for their participation in the Boer War in Southern Africa. He also took after the McKinley administration for its apparent imperialism in the Philippines which he describes as "land-stealing and liberty-crucifying." For the latter tirade he was himself accused of being a traitor for not having gone himself to fight in the Philippines.[3] He defended himself from the accusation by drawing a distinction between acting when one's country's life is in danger and supporting a war of aggression in an area far removed from its borders. Treason he defined as behavior calculated

---

2 Quoted by Philip S. Foner, *Mark* Twain: *Social Critic*, 317.
3 Foner, 359.

to deny liberty and threaten the life of one's own people or nation. True patriotism means the avoidance of wars of aggression and material exploitation, and includes criticizing one's own country whenever such aggressive policies are pursued. Twain expresses treason and patriotism negatively, according to his own version of pragmatism,[4] and in terms of the denial of liberty and the exploitation of material resources. In his opinion the New Zealand monument was neither a celebration of liberty nor of genuine patriotism.

A similar ambiguity also plagues the "telos" or purpose of the Statue of Liberty. It is generally assumed that its purpose is to celebrate and promote the liberty of all peoples, but particularly, as Emma Lazarus' poem suggests, the hopes of all the immigrants yearning to enter the "golden door" of democracy in order to "breathe free." Millions have sympathized with Lazarus' feelings for the poor, the tired, the huddled masses, the wretched, the homeless, and the tempest-tost, but still one can't help wondering how consistent these feelings are with past and current U.S. Immigration and Naturalization laws and policies. Even now persons with communicable diseases are refused admission as are all known felons, and indeed a controversy rages regarding whether legal as well as illegal immigrants from Mexico and elsewhere have had a deleterious effect on the availability of American jobs and the economy as a whole.[5]

Furthermore, immigration and naturalization from the time of the first federal statute governing these matters[6] has never been "race or sex neutral." Only white male persons could become naturalized citizens,[7] and

---

4   For an analysis of Twain's "negative pragmatism," see Davis, *Comparative Philosophy*, 177-8, 189, n.15 (where it is compared with William E. Hocking's version).

5   Many recent studies have indicated, on the contrary, that the influx of laborers and farm workers has been beneficial to the economy.

6   The U.S. Constitution merely states that Congress shall have the power "to establish an uniform Rule of Naturalization." Art. 1, § 8, although it does employ the expression "natural born citizen" in Art. 2 regarding the presidency, and in Amendment XIV speaks of "born or naturalized citizens." Jefferson as Secretary of State drafted the first statute of 1790 which was but a copy of one he had previously drafted for the legislature of Virginia.

7   At the time, if the statute had included non-whites, slaves and Indians, or women who did not yet have the vote, both the Virginia statute and the statute Jefferson drafted for the U.S. Congress probably would not have passed.

the restriction regarding white persons was in effect, almost unbelievably, until the McCarran-Walter Act of 1952 which lifted the racial restriction but kept a quota system in place. Chinese and other Asians were excluded from naturalization by legislation in 1882 and 1917.

Jefferson's 1790 statute set the residency requirement at two years. The naturalization Act of 1795 changed that to five years, and the Act of 1798, passed during the presidency of John Adams, raised it to fourteen years, for the purely political reason of reducing the number of Irish and French immigrants who were more likely to vote for the republican/democratic party of Jefferson rather than for the federalists. That maneuver was nullified when in 1802 Jefferson as President managed to repeal the Alien and Sedition Act of which the Naturalization Statute was a part. The residency requirement reverted to five years.

The Fourteenth Amendment of 1868 made "all persons born or naturalized in the United States" citizens, and granted them "equal protection of the laws." Even so naturalization was not extended to Asians until 1898, and it was not until 1943 after the repeal of the Chinese Exclusion Act of 1882 were all Asians allowed to become naturalized citizens. American Indians, although born in this land before it became a nation, and in no need of naturalization, were not granted citizen status as a class[8] until an Indian Citizenship bill was passed in 1924. Enslaved Blacks, at the time of the signing of the Constitution, for the purpose of determining representation in Congress, were each treated as if only 3/5th of a person. This restriction was rescinded by the Fourteenth Amendment, § 2, and they were given the right to vote by Amendment XV (1870). Women were finally given the federal right to vote[9] by Amendment XIX in 1920.

Thus it is abundantly clear that opening Lazarus' "golden door" was for many classes and races of prospective immigrants seeking to become American citizens a very tortuous process. However, we should not get

---

8 Some Indians were granted citizenship status earlier on condition that they subscribe to the Dawes' redistribution of Indian lands scheme. For more on this subject see Davis, *The Scalping of the Great Sioux Nation,* 80, 85.

9 Some states, Wyoming being the first, granted women suffrage (at least in state elections) before the Amendment was passed which gave them the right to vote nationally.

the impression that the Founding Fathers, and Jefferson in particular, were anti-immigrant. Most of them were either immigrants themselves or, like Jefferson, a descendant of immigrants. So when Jefferson in his First Annual Message to the Senate and the House of Representatives spoke of naturalization, they knew perfectly well what he was talking about and what is more, probably sympathized with what he had to say, which incidentally, is not so different in concept or in tone from Emma Lazarus' poem.

> And shall we refuse the unhappy fugitives from distress that hospitality which the savages of the wilderness extended to our fathers arriving in this land? Shall oppressed humanity find no asylum on this globe? The constitution, indeed, has wisely provided that, for admission to certain offices of important trust, a residence shall be required sufficient to develop character and design. But might not the general character and capabilities of a citizen be safely communicated to every one manifesting a *bona fide* purpose of embarking his life and fortunes permanently with us? with restrictions, perhaps, to guard against the fraudulent usurpation of our flag.[10]

In numerous contexts Jefferson expresses his approval of admitting foreigners to citizenship in both of his "countries" (Virginia and the U. S. A.). Somewhat curiously, but just as emphatically, he usually couples his approval, not only with certain restrictions, but with what he often describes as a right to divest oneself of such citizenship. In his *Autobiography* he says

> I prepared and obtained leave to bring in a bill declaring who should be deemed citizens, asserting *the natural right of ex-patriation,* and prescribing the mode of exercising it.[11]

---

10 Jefferson, *First Annual Message,* Peterson, 108.
11 Jefferson, *Autobiography,* Peterson, 36. Italics mine.

In the Virginia bill he says,

> The free white inhabitants of every of the states, parties
> to the American confederation, paupers[12], vagabonds, and
> fugitives from justice excepted, shall be intitled (*viz.*) to all
> rights, privileges, and immunities of free citizens of this
> commonwealth, *and shall have free egress, and regress, to and
> from the same . . .*[13]

On the one hand, he seems as anxious as Emma Lazarus to offer "unhappy
refugees" and "oppressed humanity" the promise of freedom from oppression and despair, and all the benefits of citizenship, but on the other he
seems just as anxious to assure them that they can give it all up any time
they want to and return or "egress" to their previous condition or other
status. But why in the world would anyone do such a thing? And why
even offer it to suffering humanity? The entire suggestion seems to contradict the message of Lady Liberty who, standing amid broken shackles and
chains at her feet (the symbols of oppression, rarely seen by visitors to the
monument) invites the refugee coming into the harbor to accept the gift
of liberty. If egressions and divestiture were as significant or important as a
new life of hope and freedom, shouldn't the statue be facing the other way
around? Or occasionally turned on a swivel?

One can only guess at Jefferson's motives for insisting on the right of
expatriation, but in his early work, "The Rights of British America," he
maintains the view that

> Our ancestors, before their emigration to America, were
> the free inhabitants of the British dominions of Europe,
> and possessed a right which nature had given to all men, of

---

12 Here Jefferson seems to differ from Lazarus' invitation to "the poor," but perhaps he only
meant those without the means of honest employment, just as he intends to exclude irresponsible
wanderers or vagabonds.

13 Jefferson, *A Bill Declaring Who Shall Be Deemed Citizens of this Commonwealth*, Peterson,
374. Italics mine.

departing from the country in which chance, not choice, has placed them, of going in quest of new habitations, and of there establishing new societies, under such laws and regulations as to them shall seem most likely to promote public happiness.[14]

He adds that their Saxon ancestors had done the same when they left northern Europe and migrated to the island of Britain. He appears to argue that the founders of America were within their "natural rights" to "egress" from Britain and cast off its oppressive rule. This may or may not have been Jefferson's rationale for the right of expatriation. However, it is perhaps relevant and significant that the United Nation's *Universal Declaration of Human Rights* does list the following as one of these rights:

Article 13

(1) Everyone has the right to freedom of movement and residence within the borders of each state.
(2) Everyone has the right to leave any country, including his own, and return to his country.

The second part of this right of movement appears to coincide exactly with Jefferson's right of expatriation. It is not altogether clear as to why this right was included in the *Declaration*, but the historical fact is that some countries have (at least in the past) restricted their citizens' travel outside their borders. This has happened in the Soviet Union. Nobel Prize winners have been denied permission to leave the country to go to Bergen, Norway to accept the prize. It was also the practice in Nazi Germany, and it may still be a practice in some totalitarian regimes today.

Of course, the reason for abandoning life in a country which offers freedom from oppression might be simply the desire for a different or better climate, working conditions, more familiar surroundings, or family

---

14 Jefferson, "The Rights of British America," Peterson, 105-6.

connections. In such a case expatriation would not be foolishly abandoning a life of freedom from oppression, but the seeking of a more positive kind of freedom, the freedom to do as you please. Jefferson was no doubt thinking of those who, finding oppression in one's adopted land as intolerable as in the "old country," were only exercising their right to reject oppression and pursue happiness wherever it could be found. Expatriation of this sort would then only be the reverse side of the same coin, so to speak, involving freedom from oppression but not a total rejection or refusal of the proffered freedom itself.

Another way in which the art and architecture of a country can and has been politicized is to restrict its subject-matter on grounds of religion. During the Middle Ages and High Renaissance when the great cathedrals of Europe were constructed, and the magnificent art of Michelangelo and Da Vinci was conceived and executed, the predominant subject-matter of art was strictly biblical or otherwise religious. A similar kind of restriction was placed on art by Islam which disallows any depiction of persons or nature and insists on the use solely of geometric designs for the construction of mosques and their interior and exterior decoration. Thus we see fantastic designs and mosaics in places such as the Alhambra in Granada, Spain and throughout the Arab and Muslim-dominated world. Occasionally one sees a tiny flower or set of flowers in their art works, but such attempts to include natural objects is (for some inscrutable reason) strictly blasphemous, as are also statues of persons, as we now know all too well because of the obliteration of the Buddhas by the Taliban mullah, Mohammed Omar, at Bamiyan in the Hindu Kush Mountains of Afghanistan.

Such attempts to "sanctify" art are traceable to the fact that in most instances such religious art is sponsored by the "dominant majority" (to use Jefferson's and Holmes' term) of those societies. As such there is nothing illegal about it, although in the case of the wanton destruction of the Buddhas, world-wide moral criticism has been provoked.

However, since those times most art and architecture of the civilized world has been for the most part secularized. Occasionally one sees in non-Islamic dominated countries art which reflects a religious motif, but such art and buildings are now relatively few in number. Frank Lloyd Wright's architecture, for example, is religion-neutral. Indeed he did accept commissions to design and build various churches and synagogues, and was very conscientious in attempting to respect religious methods of worship and their need of certain religious symbols. In no way, however, do his designs make an attempt to redirect or change the worshippers' convictions. Some architecture as we saw in connection with our discussion of Nazi architecture adorned with the swastika, may have had the capacity to achieve such results, but no such "telos" is detectable in Wright's religious structures.

Still another way in which contemporary art and architecture has been "politicized" is by means of what is called the "privatization" of public art. It consists of using public lands, public space or buildings, or some public art object, such as a piece of sculpture, a building, landscape, park, cartoon, or parade for private, commercial, and usually monetary ends. It involves a political act of directing persons away from the "telos" or purpose for which the land, space, or object was originally intended to some person's or corporation's private end, whatever that may be, whether increased sales, gathering opinions, affecting certain attitudes, creating certain desires, or causing certain kinds of behavior.

Examples of such privatization include the use of the Statue of Liberty as the backdrop for television advertisements promoting the Liberty Mutual Insurance Company; the use of pictures of the Presidential faces on Mount Rushmore and a cartoon gecko to promote the sales of Geico Insurance policies; or again, the use of the Peanuts cartoon character, Charlie Brown, which has become practically a public icon, to sell Metropolitan Life policies.

But there are a plethora of other somewhat different examples, such as the case of the speech given by the CEO of the Coca-Cola Company at a Naturalization ceremony held on July 4, 2011 at Jefferson's Monticello. The speech was magnificent and full of excellent advice for the new citizens, but it was also accompanied by free bottles of coke, and fans displaying on one side "Pursuit of Happiness" and on the reverse side in large unmistakable letters "Coca-Cola." Other examples include artistically designed parades on certain cordoned-off public streets in cities such as New York, Pasadena, and Minneapolis: the Macy's Thanksgiving Day Parade, the Rosebowl Parade, and the Aquatennial Parade. What is the aim of all these attempts to create magnificent floats and festivals and displaying them on admittedly public property? Quite apparently to attract more buyers of the products advertised and more customers to the local stores!

Similar privatizing has occurred in our Public School Systems by allowing private groups with their own sometimes eccentric ideas about education to run so-called "Charter Schools" or "Home Schools." Major athletic events are held in publicly-funded stadiums and arenas, baseball, football, and soccer parks, and hockey rinks. They are routinely surrounded by and plastered with advertisements shouting "Visa," Visa," "Visa," or "Goodyear," "Goodyear," "Goodyear," or "Pepsi-cola," "Pepsi-cola," Pepsi-cola," or "McDonalds," "McDonalds," "McDonalds," etc., etc., etc.

What, if anything, is wrong with such privatization, particularly as it applies to public art? As long as the private users of public property do not deliberately attempt to deceive the public, make egregiously false claims, or provoke their fans or prospective customers to destroy the property (as occasionally happens in huge assemblies, sporting events, and parades) there is really nothing criminal in these acts of politicization and/or privatization. On the other hand, critics of such privatization claim that there are more subtle aspects of these acts which are nonetheless subversive of basic democratic values. For example, often the attempt is made to exclude certain kinds of people—the poor, the indigent, or even the average low income person—from attending the events sponsored. To reach the public site at which the sponsored event or showing is being held it is sometimes necessary to own an automobile. Often even sidewalks are made generally impassable or unusable by such "down-market" people, who are supposed to have the same rights as the rest of us. At other times the art displayed for public consumption is in bad taste, e.g., the "Forever Marilyn" statue, or it is offensive to certain residential communities, e.g., a neo-Nazi parade down the streets of a predominantly Jewish community, or a parade of the

KKK down the streets of Washington, D. C. Sometimes the public has a say about permitting such events, but sometimes they do not.

Sometimes the fee or price one is required to pay to view whatever is occurring on public land or space is exorbitantly high in order to filter out certain members of the society, and there is nothing government officials can do about it. Access by the elderly or the crippled is thwarted by the lack of ramps or elevators, although most states by law now require such methods of access. Charter schools, although licensed by the government and inspected occasionally to assure minimum standards are nonetheless free to introduce materials and practices which are usually not permitted in public schools. Parochial schools, some of which receive public grants, are similarly allowed to instill religious doctrines in their students.

Given all these practices of subverting public property to private goals, one wonders whatever happened to the Separation of Church & State doctrine, and more generally what has happened to the distinctions between Public Art and Non-Public Art, Democracy and Autocracy, or Democracy and Oligarchy? If indeed privatization leads to such political consequences, and admittedly this is still an arguable matter, then no pragmatist can accept it, since with such social practices, society in the long run will not be better off.

Chapter VI

IS PUBLIC ART/ARCHITECTURE PROPAGANDA? SHOULD IT AIM AT UPGRADING MORAL AND AESTHETIC STANDARDS? IS AMUSEMENT OR PLEASURE A GOAL OF PUBLIC ART?

The word, "propaganda" comes from the Latin word "propagare" meaning to disseminate. Thus the usual morally-neutral definition is something like "a doctrine or plan for the dissemination of ideas," or " a systematic effort to persuade a people of a certain set of ideas or to adopt a certain attitude." Historically, a *College of Propaganda* was instituted by Urban VIII (1623-44) to educate priests before going on religious missions. More recently the term has acquired a more negative and morally offensive meaning, namely, the promotion of false and duplicitous claims or views.

We have already discussed several instances of the propagandistic uses of public art and architecture, such as the New Zealand monument meant to extol the loyalty and patriotism of a few Maori tribesmen whom Mark Twain viewed as traitors. The alleged duplicity is painfully obvious in that case. Not so with regard to the Statue of Liberty, although even here the gap between the freedom from oppression which Emma Lazarus offers when she says "Give me your tired, your poor, your huddled masses yearning to breathe free," and the actual requirements for naturalization, makes one wonder just how genuine the offer of freedom which Lady Liberty symbolizes really is, and whether this constitutes an instance of propaganda.

However, we have also discussed cases in which even this last hint of propaganda does not appear to exist. Take Michelangelo's *David*. Today at least, although it extols political courage, there seems to be no duplicity or ugly propaganda in its display. Also consider Jefferson's life-long effort to upgrade his Monticello residence. If we set aside all attempts to give it a hidden Freudian sexual interpretation,[1] it would appear that his efforts only reflect two motives, the first to satisfy his own high architectural standards, and second to educate the public at large regarding good architecture. As he indicated to James Madison,

> You see I am an enthusiast on the subject of the arts. But it is an enthusiasm of which I am not ashamed, as its object is to improve the taste of my countrymen, to increase their reputation, to reconcile to them the respect of the world, and procure them its praise.[2]

In that letter he was referring specifically to his attempt to get the Virginia Legislature to construct their new State House on the model of the Maison Carré (Jefferson spells it *quarrée)* at Nîsmes, France, but by implication also to Monticello. Regarding architectural education generally he says,

> But how is a taste in this beautiful art to be formed in our countrymen, unless we avail ourselves of every occasion when public buildings [or private] are to be erected, of presenting them models for their study and imitation?[3]

It is not particularly difficult to see how Hitler sought to educate the German people about their being *"Uber Alles,"* that is, superior to all others

---

1   Cf. below, 18. Even Freud said that sometimes a cigar is only a cigar, so the sexual allegations are perhaps not even the results of correct Freudian analysis.

2   TJ to James Madison, Sept. 20, 1785. Peterson, 830.

3   Ibid., Peterson, 829.

through the medium of his gigantic public buildings, monuments, and arenas. Nor is it difficult to see how a memorial to Lincoln, the "Great Emancipator," is meant to educate Americans about the evils of slavery and the importance of human freedom in a democracy. But there are other forms of public art where the educational intent or benefit is less clear. Take what is generally referred to as pornographic, erotic, or obscene art. Pornography is for the most part concerned only with graphic or written art—these days especially with internet presentations—and so not usually lumped together with public art. Although the problems with it are very similar to those affecting public art per se (if we may refer to it in that manner). we shall by-pass any direct discussion of it. Erotic art involving statuary and other decorative features of architecture will be our main focus here.

One of the main problems related to eroticism is clarifying the distinction between being nude and being naked. Another is determining why certain natural human acts or activities, such as fornication, urination, defecation, which are customarily performed privately, are suddenly to be classed as erotic and/or obscene[4] when presented publicly in the form of art. (These can of course also be expressed graphically, in painting and writing, and so fall also within the category of pornography). First let us consider nudity as it occurs in public art.

Certainly the portrayal of the nude human body has been done by artists from Paleolithic times through the Classical Greek and Roman periods of sculptural art to the present day. Pick almost any artist, sculptor, or architect and you will discover among his works some effort to depict the nude human body, whether male or female. Even the most religiously minded artist, other than the orthodox Muslim, of course, has so indulged him or herself, and with Biblical justification. How else could one properly and accurately depict Adam and Eve? Given this history, it is not at all surprising that the U. S. Supreme Court has held that no work of art

---

4 There is an almost inescapable ambiguity here. Many artists claim that art can be erotic without being obscene, whereas many other persons, including religionists and some jurists, maintain that all erotic art is obscene.

is to be regarded as obscene merely because the human body is displayed unclothed or nude.[5]

In *Roth v. United States* (354 U. S. 476), decided in 1957, the Court adopted a rule which defined obscenity as "material whose dominant theme taken as a whole appeals to prurient interest" to "the average person, applying contemporary community standards." To be classed as obscene a work of art (in this particular case, a work of literature) it had to be shown to (1) appeal to prurient interests; (2) be patently offensive; and (3) have no redeeming social value. Almost a decade later in 1966, in the case of *Memoirs v. Massachusetts* (383 U. S. 413), the Court decided that the book *Fanny Hill,* also known as *Memoirs of a Woman of Pleasure,* could not be proscribed by the criminal statutes of Massachusetts because, although it met the first two requirements, it was not shown to have met the third.

In 1964, in the case of *Jacobelli v. Ohio* (318 U. S. 184) Justice Potter Stewart expressed his dissatisfaction with the Roth rule, and in his attempt to explain obscenity in art confessed: "I shall not today attempt today to define the kinds of materials I understand to be embraced . . . but I know it when I see it." Later in 1973, in *Miller v. California* (413 U.S. 15) Chief Justice Warren E. Burger argued for and obtained, by a 5-4 vote, a somewhat "looser" definition of obscenity which would make prosecutions for obscenity easier. It overruled the tests used in the *Roth* and *Memoirs* cases and set up the following criteria to be met before State intervention and prohibition was legitimate: (1) an average person would find that the work, taken as a whole, appeals to a lewd curiosity; (2) the work depicts, in an offensive way, sexual conduct or excretory functions; and (3) the work, taken as a whole, lacks serious literary, artistic, political, or scientific value. No longer need the Court find that the art work was utterly without redeeming social value. Although among the minority on the Court, Justice William J. Brennan held out for the view that the First Amendment protects all obscenity except that distributed to minors or exposed offensively to unconsenting adults.

---

5 See *Jenkins v. Georgia,* 418 U.S. 153 (1974).

During the 1960's and early 1970's the homoerotic and sadomasochistic art of Robert Mapplethorpe (1946-1989) was the subject of controversy and multiple lawsuits. Somewhat later the photography of Andres Serrano became the focus, particularly because of an art work called "Piss Christ" (1987) in which a plastic crucifix is shown submerged in what is allegedly his own urine. Senator Jesse Helms attacked the work as offensive art, but the artist was defended by the New York Times citing the need for and importance of artistic freedom. When shown at an art gallery in Lund, Sweden, in 2007, his art works were vandalized by persons thought to be neo-Nazis carrying out Hitler's attack on what he and they regarded as "degenerate" art. Serrano's "Piss Christ" piece when shown in Avignon, France, was vandalized by a group of French Catholic fundamentalists. The work was sold at auction for $277,000.

Given the extent of disagreement over what is obscene and what isn't, and the difficulties of providing a clear cut definition, whether it be obscenity in painting. literature, photography, sculpture, or architecture (there is much exotic and arguably obscene decoration in the art and architecture of India), what is to be the pragmatist's perspective on all these matter? Quite obviously the pragmatic philosopher/art critic is in no position to dictate what is to be accepted in law as obscene or not obscene. Nor does the pragmatist critic think that that is his task. Rather, in keeping with the experimentalism and futuristic consequentialism of pragmatism, his position has to be that all the competing theories should be given their chance to promote the best interests of society. Those conceptions which prove to be deleterious should be rejected and only then outlawed.

But is the test of what is in the "best interests of society" what pleases the dominant majority, or in the language of *Roth*, what is consistent with "contemporary community standards"? Negatively expressed, does this mean that all art which displeases the dominant majority or violates contemporary community standards be either condemned as obscene (bad or unchaste) art, or regarded as not even art at all? It seems doubtful that even a democratically-minded pragmatist could accept such a test. One has to remember that much of the art which Hitler treated as "degenerate" is today regarded by all the world as superlative, even though perhaps the dominant majority in Nazi culture at the time disapproved it. And why should the U. S. Senate or influential Senators such as Jesse Helms or others have the final say with respect to the obscenity or the legitimacy of Serrano's art when even the *New York Times* defended it? And doesn't it make sense, as the defendant in *Miller* argued, that a national rather than a merely local community standard for obscenity be applied to his and other cases? Miller did not call for a "universal" standard, and since pragmatists are practically and empirically oriented, not to do so makes eminently good sense, even though Justice O. W. Holmes, himself a pragmatist, when speaking to a group of law students, once said

> The remoter and more general aspects of the law are those which give it universal interest. It is through them that you only become a great master in your calling, but connect your subject with the universe, and catch an echo of the infinite, a glimpse of its unfathomable process, a hint of the universal law.[6]

To a great extent the fierce disagreement over what is obscene art or architecture results because of several confusions or misconceptions regarding which the pragmatist may have something relevant to say. The first confusion involves the identification of good art with pleasant art, or more generally of the good with the pleasant. Many persons regard bad art as simply art which doesn't please, amuse, or entertain them. The second confusion which derives from the first is that art *is* simply a form of amusement, or to use Santayana's phrase, a case of "objectified pleasure." The third confusion is that art is some kind of useless object,[7] rather than a special activity or function.

---

6 Holmes, "The Path of the Law," in Max Lerner, *The Mind and Faith of Justice Holmes*, 89.

7 William James, who knew better, nonetheless says in his *Psychology: The Briefer Course*, xxviii, that "The study of the harmful [in mental life] has been made the subject of a special branch called Psychiatry . . . and the study of the useless is made over to Aesthetics."

Historically there have been many attempts to equate the good with the pleasant, and the bad with the unpleasant or painful. All such simpleminded hedonistic attempts have failed since there are so many phenomena which cannot be fully described in those terms, even if the notion of goodness is expanded to include the utilitarian notion of "greatest happiness." As William James once put it,

> Take the love of drunkenness; take bashfulness, the terror of high places, the tendency to seasickness, to faint at the sight of blood, the susceptibility to musical sounds; take the emotion of the comical, the passion for poetry, for mathematics, or for metaphysics—no one of these things can we wholly explain [or justify] by either association or utility.[8]

The confusion of the good with the pleasant often occurs because pleasant consequences frequently *accompany* good acts, but not always. There really is such a thing as unrequited love, ingratitude for benefits received, and disdain returned for generosity. And so we find it also in art. Sometimes art isn't pleasant to view, listen to, touch, or participate in, and yet the art product may very well measure up to the highest standards. It is often heavily dependent on personal preferences and/or prejudices. To some minds "Piss Christ" may seem appalling, blasphemous, and contemptible, but the fact is that someone was willing to buy it at auction for $277,000. Other persons may regard "Forever Marilyn" as pure kitsch and suitable only for the garbage dump, but the fact of the matter is that the City Fathers of Palm Springs welcomed it with open arms as a significant and attractive public art object. Given such a disparity in persons' views, it seems utterly dogmatic to insist that the only good art is art which produces pleasure.

From this confusion arises another and more far reaching one, the view that art is simply a form of amusement. It is more far reaching because it not only encompasses pleasant matters but also allows for the fact that

---

8 James, "The Moral Philosopher and the Moral Life," in *Essays in Faith and Morals,* , 186-87.

art often deals with fearful situations, bloody war scenes, amputated body parts, ugly nakedness and acts of sexual deviance. How often do such depictions grasp our attention, or appeal to our "lewd curiosity," or make us fearful? Think of the many persons who choose to ride roller coasters at Amusement Parks solely for the sheer fear which those rides engender. And how many perfectly respectable and well educated persons have been ashamed to admit that they have been attracted to scenes of horror (in real life as well as in the movies) to the extent that they cannot take their eyes off them? How many persons have found "Forever Marilyn" or other depictions of naughty behavior interesting and entertaining? There are an enormous number of such shameful and devious acts and objects which, as often as not, provoke our interest and amuse us. Perhaps we shouldn't be so susceptible to such provocations or indulgences, but human beings are peculiar creatures. Thus it isn't at all surprising that art which portrays the ugly or the unpleasant should also intrigue, amuse, and entertain us.

Still, the conclusion that art is therefore simply a form of amusement rests on two serious confusions, first regarding the motives for viewing or studying art; and second, regarding the aesthetic experience one may have while doing so. Regarding motives, no one chooses to visit a museum, sculpture garden, or skyscraper complex such as the Rockefeller Center, or the Empire State Building for the same reasons one might choose to attend a movie or a theatrical performance. In the latter cases we are seeking entertainment, but in the former something else seems to be involved. What could that be? Perhaps a specific example will help. As every parent knows, children, especially when school is out, need a diversion of some kind. My two daughters therefore once decided to take their children to the Smithsonian Museum of American History, and upon entering were told by the receptionist to be sure to see Dorothy's red shoes which were used in *The Wizard of Oz,* and other paraphernalia from that artistic production. The children were indeed interested and undoubtedly entertained by these observations, but that had not been their primary motive for visiting the museum. Like others who attend museums, they were seeking, and in this particular case did see "original" art objects. Most persons would agree that seeing the original rather than a copy is worth the effort of going to a public museum. Seeing Michelangelo's *David* and not a mere replica of it is well worth the trip to Florence. But is that satisfaction fully explained as amusement or entertainment? Certainly not. Seeking out the original may or may not please the observer. The actual painting of Leonardo da Vinci's *Mona* Lisa may appear to some to be much smaller than might have been expected, and so somewhat disappointing. In the cases of Dorothy's shoes and Michelangelo's David, they did please the observers, but that is almost beside the point, and usually does not account for the actual motive for seeking them out.

Or take still another case. Suppose one is given the opportunity to view Michelangelo's *Pieta* sculpture up close, and to marvel at the absolute genius it took to create the work. One might under such circumstances be humbled by the piety it expresses, or have an experience one might characterize as religious, but might it also be described as "entertaining" or "amusing"? Never! But if so this brings us to still another confusion regarding what counts as an aesthetic experience.

We are accustomed to thinking of art in terms of the so-called "art object." Thus art is that portrait or picture hanging on the wall of a museum, or that building on the corner of the block, or that monument or statue erected in the City Park, or that Parade down Main Street. Even though observing the painting or portrait involves visiting a museum; examining a building or other piece of architecture requires walking through it or touching parts of it; enjoying a parade entails going to it, standing beside it or sometimes even being in it, we often think we have really not viewed its artistic features until we have "captured" it on film by "taking" its picture. The object somehow has to be a kind of thing perceived directly by our senses, what epistemologists would describe as a "sense-datum," essentially not much different from a "still-life," and in itself perfectly useless. To view art in such a manner is, in effect, to siphon off all the activity associated with it and all its functionality. No pragmatist could possibly tolerate such a position.

But let us examine this viewpoint more minutely. Are we to say, and literally mean, that art is not a kind of thing or object? Take the most obvious cases where art seems to be an object of some kind—a painting by Picasso, framed and hanging on the wall, or a building constructed of glass and steel, situated on or by a country "run," say, Frank Lloyd Wright's *Fallingwater*. Consider the painting first. Which sense image (or "sense-datum") will provide us with the art object, the painting seen closeup or the painting viewed at a distance? Some paintings seen closeup appear to be only smears of colored pigment, or if viewed from too far away as not resembling any identifiable thing. So also for a building such as *Fallingwater*. Viewed at night its cubist features are particularly evident, and under various weather conditions or when the stream beneath isn't running, it looks much different. This phenomenon is certainly true also for many an architectural structure. Which sense-datum is supposed to be "the art object"? It is patently clear that if one adopted this sense-datum or "thing theory" of art, one might become convinced that art is indeed pretty useless, not that anyone would be willing to admit that paintings could have any effects on the feelings or emotions of those who view them, or that building aren't useful in directing traffic (as even the Nazis discovered), or that gardens (particularly Japanese gardens) aren't designed to excite the senses or relax the soul, but if the art is only a thing sensed (like the color Blue) and nothing more, these functions have to be regarded as irrelevancies.

Now having disposed, we hope, of the view that the primary goal of art is pleasure, that art is a kind of amusement, and that art is a kind of useless sense-datum (like blue) or mere object of perception, we next need to examine in a more positive fashion what are the "material causes" of art, and the real nature of the aesthetic experience.

Chapter VII

WHAT ARE THE MATERIAL CAUSES OF ART AND AESTHETIC EXPERIENCE? DOES DEWEY'S THEORY MEET THE PRAGMATIC CRITERIA? DOES PUBLIC ART HAVE A HISTORY? COLLINGWOOD'S VIEW

From an empiricist's, and therefore also from a pragmatist's, point of view, the materials of art are the common objects and events of human experience, or in a word, nature or the world at large. That does not mean that that everything humanly experienced is an actual or even potentially an art object. The artist, whether painter, musician, architect, or sculptor, chooses as his or her subject matter some specific part, aspect, or place in this world and from these parts, aspects, and places, creates art. The painter uses paints, the musician sounds, the sculptor stones, granite, or marble, and the architect, bricks, boards, steel, glass, and concrete.

This account of the "material causes" of art seems so commonsensical and so obviously platitudinous that it should hardly be necessary even to verbalize it, and yet many theories of art reject it as a proper analysis of the "stuff," so to speak, of art. At one extreme there is the view of the pure formalist who totally objects to the notion that art has anything at all to do with nature as such, or the world as experienced by human beings. Clive Bell, the most notorious representative of this point of view puts it this way:

To appreciate a work of art we need bring with us nothing from life, no knowledge of its ideas and affairs, no familiarity with its emotions. Art transports us from the world of man's activity to a world of esthetic exaltation. . . . The rapt philosopher, and he who con-templates a work of art, inhabit a world with an intense and peculiar significance of its own; that significance is unrelated to the significance of life. In this world the emotions of life find no place. It is a world with emotions of its own.[1]

According to Bell, the basic matter or material of art is what he calls "pure," "created" or "significant" form.

Before a work of art people who feel little or no emotion for pure form find themselves at a loss. They are deaf men at a concert . . .And so they read into the forms of the work those facts and ideas for which they are capable of feeling emotion. . . the ordinary emotions of life. When confronted by a picture, instinctively they refer back its forms to the world from which they came. They treat created form as though it were imitated form, a picture as though it were a photograph. . . . To use art as a means to the emotions of life is to use a telescope for reading the news.[2]

For a person capable of seeing the created form in art, and experiencing genuine aesthetic emotions (as opposed to ordinary emotions), Bell contends that "a good work of visual art carries a person . . . out of life into ecstasy."[3] Furthermore, they often

1 Clive Bell, *Art*, 27-28.
2 Ibid., 29.
3 Ibid.

have no idea what the subject of the picture is. They have never noticed the representative element, and so when they discuss pictures they talk about the shapes of forms and the relations and quantities of colors. Often they can tell by the quality of a single line whether or not a man is a good artist. They are concerned only with lines and colors, their relations and quantities[4]

Thomas Jefferson, as we have already observed, was something of a formalist as far as the art of architecture is concerned. He insisted that unless a structure was consistent with Palladian rules, it could not be "beautiful" or "right." Thus he concluded that in the Williamsburg of his time the Capitol was "the most pleasing piece of architecture that we have," even though it did not completely measure up to Palladian standards, and that the Lunatic Hospital, which he thought better resembled a brick kiln and was in no way constructed in accordance with Palladian rules, was not even art.

On the other hand, he also valued convenience and accommodating environmental location as well as form. These factors distinguish his view from Bell's which places its total emphasis, as far as the matter and materials of art is concerned, on "created form," or as he also says, "significant form." In this respect, and in partial defense of Bell's contention, it must be noted that everything in nature has some form or other, but that fact doesn't make those objects art, or the emotions they inspire aesthetic experiences. Take for example the aurora borealis or a glorious sunset which provide the observer with bursts of color and certain natural forms. It can be awe inspiring but a sunset itself is not an "art object" nor is the experience of it an artistic experience, although perhaps it is aesthetic in a much larger sense of that term. Insofar as art is concerned with forms they must be "created forms," involving human agency as Bell has insisted, and most philosophers of art would probably go along with him on this point.

---

4 Ibid. 29-30.

At the other extreme, however, with respect to the material causes of art and architecture, is the view that it is not something in the things of nature such as their forms, colors, etc. which is the primary stuff of art, but it is rather something in the manner in which those things are viewed, in our consciousness or our experiences of them, that is the key factor which makes them art objects and our awareness of them aesthetic experiences. Views such as these are generally classified as "expressionist" theories.

There are several ambiguities related to these theories which urgently need to be cleared up. First, whose expressions or conscious experience is to count as the art object, that of the artist or that of the art observer? Second, if the art object (or material cause of the art) is some kind of expression, what exactly is expressed— some thought or emotion in the mind of the artist (whether sculptor, painter, musician, or architect), or some thought or emotion in the mind of the observer or inspector of the art?

If one were to attempt to give a complete and thorough analysis or understanding of a piece of art, or artwork, undoubtedly one would have to attempt not only to try to decide what was the artist's intention—literally what was in his mind when he took his chisel or t-square in hand—but also what was the artist's plan or design. But these are tasks regarding the formal and efficient causes of the art, not with its material cause, which is what we are here concerned with. Even if we could answer these questions satisfactorily, which without some verbal suggestions by the artist himself might be quite impossible, we would learn only something about the artist, the efficient cause, but little or nothing about what was actually expressed or the presumed art object itself. And if that is not, as Bell claims, a "created form" of some kind, then what is its content?

Many philosophers such as R. G. Collingwood, Benedetto Croce, George Santayana, and John Dewey have attempted to answer that question. Instead of examining the whole range of expressionist views—from the theory that the art object, or primary focus of aesthetic experience, is the emotion or feeling portrayed in and through the art materials, or the emotions evoked in the consumer or viewer of the art by the historical or aesthetic imagination, or, as Santayana puts it, the projection of "objectified pleasure"—let us concentrate on John Dewey's expressionist view, primarily to see whether his account of what he calls "art as experience" accords with the general tradition of pragmatism.

A warning, however, must be given to the reader, however, for not only is Dewey's theory far more complicated and profound than all the other simpler versions of expressionism, his manner of explicating it is very challenging and at times appears almost opaque. Thomas M. Alexander has described reading Dewey like "swimming through oatmeal."[5] Typical examples are the following, both from the chapter on art in Dewey's book, *Experience and Nature:*

> Art in being, the active productive process, may thus be defined as an esthetic perception together with an *operative* perception of the efficiencies of the esthetic object.

Or again, on the very next page,

> Without a sense of moving tendencies which are operative in conjunction with a state of fruition, there is appetitive gratification, but nothing that may be termed appreciation.[6]

When Dewey's magnum opus in aesthetics, *Art As Experience,* came out, it was criticized by Stephen Pepper, later a staunch advocate of Dewey, and Benedetto Croce, a devotee of Hegelian idealist philosophy. Both thought that Dewey had reverted to a more or less idealist position which he had held when younger. The basis of their claim was that in *Art As Experience* Dewey emphasized the organic or wholistic character of the aesthetic experience by combining not only the thoughts, intentions, and emotions of the artist with the thoughts and emotions of the observer, but also by emphasizing the relation of art to the environment. They cited certain statements by Dewey to the effect that works of art prove our "belonging to the larger,

---

5 Alexander, *John Dewey's Theory of Art, Experience and Nature: The Horizons of Feeling,* xii.
6 Dewey, *Experience and Nature,* Ch. IX, 375-76.

all inclusive whole which is the universe in which we live." Such declarations, they maintained, suggest a kind of idealistic thinking as opposed to a more pragmatically oriented perception. Pepper was quite blunt in asserting that Dewey had, at least in this department of his thinking, given up pragmatism.

In fact he had done nothing of the kind, and rather forcibly said so in his replies to these critics, [7] declaring that the idealist in any case had no monopoly on words such as "whole, complete, coherence, integration, etc." His organic, wholistic (or holistic), approach is implicit in much pragmatic philosophy. Take for example William James, and his notion of the "entire"[8] or "whole man."

> Pretend what we may, the whole man within us is at work when we form our philosophical opinions. Intellect, will, taste, and passion co-operate just as they do in practical affairs.[9]

Morton G. White, a former student of Dewey at Columbia University and later an adherent of his general point of view, uses James' "whole man" thesis as the basis of his own philosophy which he calls "Holistic Pragmatism."[10] Consider also James' wholistic notion of consciousness as a "stream of experience" as opposed to the sensationalistic empiricist notion of experience, best expressed by David Hume, as a collection of essentially disconnected ideas and impressions. Dewey explicitly and approvingly refers to "James' comparison of the course of consciousness to a stream" and his rejection of the disconnectedness of sensationalistic empiricism.[11] Also when speaking specifically about aesthetic criticism, Dewey says,

---

7 See Dewey, "Experience, Knowledge and Values: A Rejoinder," in *The Philosophy of John Dewey,* ed. Paul Arthur Schilpp, 2nd ed..

8 James, "The Sentiment of Rationality," 7

9 Ibid., 24.

10 White, *A Philosophy of Culture,* 1.

11 Dewey, *Experience and Nature,* 312; *Logic: The Theory of Inquiry,* 518, n.1

> When criticism ... [is] distinguished from appreciation, ...
> we are in the presence of one case of the constant rhythm
> of "perchings and flights" (to borrow James' terms) char-
> acteristic of the alternate emphasis upon . . . the con-
> summatory and instrumental phases of all conscious
> experience.[12]

Reciprocally James for his part wholly agrees with Dewey's "instrumental-
ism," thus reinforcing the notion of human experience as a unified entity
but one which permits transference from one part (or "perching") to another in a practical way. As James puts it,

> Any idea upon which we can ride, so to speak; any idea
> that will carry us prosperously from any one part of our
> experience to any other part, linking things satisfactorily,
> working securely, simplifying, saving labor; is true for just
> so much, true in so far forth, true *instrumentally*. This is
> the "instrumental" view of truth taught so successfully at
> Chicago [where Dewey was professor at the time].[13]

It has at times been suggested that there is a strand of idealism in pragmatism, and considering James' frequent and favorable references to his idealistic colleague, Josiah Royce's views, and to the views of George Berkeley,
that claim may in fact be true, but if there is some overlap of views, the
source thereof among classical philosophers is more likely to be Berkeley's
version of idealism rather than Hegel's.

Granted therefore that for Dewey art is some kind of unified experience, which he often speaks of as *an experience,* can we determine from his
definition of art given above (p. 96) in *Experience and Nature,* which we

---

12 Dewey, *Experience and Nature,* 400. 1
13 James, "What Pragmatism Means"

found so difficult to understand, and from another in *Art As Experience*,[14] which has been detected by Thomas Leddy in his book *The Extraordinary in the Ordinary*,[15] what else is included in his conception? Let us then examine his statement that art is an "esthetic perception," an active productive process which includes certain "operative efficiencies" and "moving tendencies."

It is regrettable that Dewey chooses to use the ordinary word, "perception" in this connection. One might get the idea that he means only to suggest that the art object or expression is a mere feeling or emotion such as that of delight or sadness, for example, but that is far from what he has in mind. Nor does Dewey mean to suggest that it is a kind of experience analogous to a religious or non-sensuous mystical experience such as Clive Bell describes which "takes us from ordinary life into a world of ecstasy." For Dewey the artistic experience is unique in its own way but also a very common human experience. Perhaps like A. N. Whitehead he should have invented his own special term. Whitehead avoided the use of the words "perception" and "apprehension" in his epistemology and replaced them with "prehension." Dewey tried rather unsuccessfully to accomplish the same sort of goal in aesthetics by means of the expression "an experience." In *Art As Experience* he says that it is unfortunate that there is no word in English which combines the notion of art production with the notion of art appreciation.[16] Instead of "perception" he might have added clarity by using either "apprehension" or "apperception," but that of course is pure speculation.

We know that Dewey intended to describe art as a unified (or integral) experience, but exactly how does such an experience differ from our usual

---

14 Dewey: "When the structure of the object is such that its force interacts happily (but not easily) with the energies that issue from the experience itself; when their mutual affinities and antagonisms work together to bring about a substance that develops cumulatively and surely (but not too steadily) toward a fulfilling of impulsions, then indeed there is a work of art." *Art As Experience*, 38.

15 Leddy, *The Extraordinary in the Ordinary: The Aesthetics of Everyday Life*, 80-81.

16 Dewey, *Art As Experience*, 46.

ordinary, generally disorganized, and as he sometimes calls it, "diffuse and inchoate" experience? In his attempt to explain, he provides us what is essentially an analogy, although he doesn't call it that. Having a genuine aesthetic experience, he suggests, is much like having "an experience" of eating a magnificent meal at a Parisian restaurant.[17] More technically, it involves both a "doing" and an "undergoing," a production and a consumption, or put still otherwise, some act by the artist coupled with some reception or appreciation by the consumer/observer. Both "elements" or "ingredients" are required in order for a proper aesthetic experience of an art object to occur.

Dewey also tries to explain the "integrity" of the aesthetic experience by reference to the end-means distinction. Before the artist begins his work, with paint brush, chisel, or T-square in hand, he has an "end-in-view" which in certain definite ways dictates the "means" (i.e., the matter, materials, tools, etc.) he or she must use to accomplish his end goal. But according to Dewey these are not altogether separable features. The end may dictate the means but the means may also influence the end.

It may be of some interest to realize that Thomas Jefferson held a similarly pragmatic view of the reciprocal relation between ends and means. Responding to a question whether an "officer of high trust" [e.g., the President] might sometimes justifiably violate a written law, Jefferson replied that

> A strict observance of the written laws is doubtless *one* of the high duties of a good citizen, but it is not *the highest*. The laws of necessity, of self-preservation, of saving our country when in danger, are of higher obligation. To lose our country by a scrupulous adherence to written law, would be to lose the law itself, with life, liberty, property, and all those who are enjoying them with us, thus absurdly sacrificing the end to the means.[18]

---

17 Ibid. 36.
18 TJ to John B. Colvin, Sept. 20, 1810. Peterson, 1231.

His remarks are primarily concerned with the distinction in connection with matters of politics and law, but it is easy to see that, given his own departures from Palladian rules of architecture, which we have previously discussed, he quite obviously thought they applied to matters of art as well.

According to Dewey, not only does the unified or integral experience which constitutes the aesthetic experience contain within it means which are pragmatically related to ends, and involve both a doing and an undergoing, it is something which the art observer must appreciate. It must also be a "consummatory" experience, without which he maintains there is no art! Dewey emphasizes that consumption may entail a lengthy process in order to be "productive." If the prospective consumer of the art has not taken the necessary time to inspect the art object, or has for some reason not been allowed to,[19] he or she will be like Bell's deaf person at a concert. Robert B. Westbrook neatly summarizes Dewey's view on this specific matter as follows.

> Dewey made a particular point of emphasizing that appreciating a work of art was as much an active, often prolonged, process as creating one. . . . But for the consummatory experience of art to be had by its audience, this audience had to bring together prior experience and imaginative insight in a fashion similar to that of the artist. . . . Appreciating art, in other words, was hard work, if not as hard as making it. One simply could not, for example, appreciate great paintings by rushing through a museum gathering up the momentary sensations they excited. Dewey himself, as his daughter-in-law noted following their trip to the museums of Leningrad in 1928, would stand for a long time in

19 A case in point: The *Book of Kells* containing its magnificent painted scrolls and designs is located in the Library of Trinity College, Dublin, Ireland, and is visited and viewed by more than 500,000 persons a year. Because its quarters are so small and the viewing public so large, one is forcibly ushered through the Library at so fast a pace that a consummatory experience in Dewey's sense is literally impossible. As a consequence no genuinely aesthetic experience of any sort is likely to take place.

intense concentration before a painting attempting to appreciate fully the experience it afforded.[20] The appreciation of art required cultivated taste. But because of the continuity between works of art and everyday experience, aesthetic appreciation was not an esoteric capacity confined to a favored few; it could be learned.[21]

Much of Dewey's theory of art, as so far discussed, makes eminently good sense, but there are still some difficult lingering questions. Suppose one has the time to have a genuine consummatory experience, what then? According to pragmatists generally, and to Oliver Wendell Holmes, Jr. specifically, "every idea is an incitement to action."[22] But where is or what is the action produced by the act of aesthetic appreciation as viewed by Dewey? Or is the consummatory experience the sole end product of the aesthetic experience?

In architecture, a carefully designed and executed entrance to a building entices a viewer to enter it. A large "royal" staircase, which Jefferson personally detested and did not incorporate into Monticello, invites a person to climb it. In a visit to Nîsmes, France, Jefferson reports that he was absolutely fascinated by what he termed "the most perfect and precious remain of antiquity in existence" whose "superiority over any thing in Rome, in Greece, at Balbec or Palmyra, is allowed on all hands"—a building in the classical style named the Maison Carrée.[23] So fascinated was he that in a letter to Madame de Tessé he admitted "gazing whole hours at the Maison quarrée [sic], like a lover at his mistress."[24] Later and as a consequence of this aesthetic experience, Jefferson was impelled to suggest that the new Capitol building, or Statehouse, in his home state of Virginia, at

---

20   Dewey, by the way was fully aware of the passage in James' *Principles of Psychology*, mentioned earlier in another connection regarding the English couple who sat for hours appreciating Titian's painting "Assumption." See *Art as Experience*, 91.

21   Roberrt B. Westbrook, *John Dewey and American Democracy*, 395. Relevant citations of Dewey omitted.

22   Holmes, *Gitlow v. N.Y.*, 206 U.S. 652 (1925), dissent reprinted in Lerner, 324.

23   *TJ to William Buchanan and Hay James Hay*, Jan. 26, 1786. Peterson, 845-46.

24   *TJ to Madame de Tessé*, Mar. 20, 1787.

Richmond, be constructed in its likeness. He would supply all the plans. It was in fact constructed in accordance with Jefferson's instructions.

In all these cases the pragmatic consequences of the aesthetic experiences are palpably demonstrated, but where in Dewey's conception do we find similar productive consequences? It is likely that he intends to include them since he speaks of aesthetics as involving a "productive process" and "efficiencies of the esthetic object" and operative "moving tendencies," but a clear delineation of them is totally missing.

Another serious ambiguity faults his theory. The consummatory integral experience which he likens to having "an experience" [of a good meal; playing a game of chess; having successfully solved a mechanical problem[25]) seems also in all, or most cases, to be equivalent to having a pleasurable one. Yet it is next to impossible to find a passage in his writings where he says so explicitly. For example,

> Modern theory has quite properly extended the application of the term [art] to cover many things that the Greeks would hardly have called "experience," the bare having of aches and pains, or a play of colors before the eyes. But even those who hold this larger signification would admit, I suppose, that such "experiences" count only when they result in insight, or in an enjoyed perception.[26]

Or again,

> In the esthetic object tendencies are sensed as brought to fruition; in it is embodied a means-consequence relationship, as the past work of his hands was surveyed by the Lord and pronounced good. . . In appreciative possession, perception goes out to tendencies which have been

25 Dewey, Art As Experience, 35.
26 Dewey, *Experience and Nature*, 354.

brought to happy fruition in such a way as to release and arouse.[27]

Although Dewey explicitly rejects the theory that art is the expression of the emotions,[28] he confounds our understanding by also saying,

> It is intelligible that art should select and assemble objective things in such ways as to evoke emotional response of a refined, sensitive and enduring kind; . . . But it still remains true that the origin of the art-process lay in emotional responses spontaneously called out by a situation occurring without any reference to art, and without "esthetic" quality save in the sense in which all immediate enjoyment and suffering is esthetic.[29]

As we have already indicated, none of the other pragmatists, such as James and Holmes (any more than the Nazis) have ever maintained that the ultimate goal of either morality or art is the production of pleasure, or even the greatest happiness (or good) of the greatest number.[30] But what else could Dewey mean when he uses terms such as "enjoyed perception," "happy fruition," or "immediate esthetic enjoyment"? He does at times insist that the aesthetic experience (as well as the art object) involves suffering and conflict, and indeed that is presumably why so many pragmatists and others do not adopt what is essentially a hedonistic theory, for much great art does depict great suffering (e.g., scenes of the Crucifixion,

---

27 Ibid., 374-75

28 Ibid., 390.

29 Ibid., 390-91

30 Cf. Holmes's statement: "Why should the greatest number be preferred? Why not the greatest good of the most intelligent and most highly developed? The greatest good of a minority of our generation may be the greatest good of the greatest number in the long run.." *The Gas Stokers' Strike,* 7 ALR 582 (1873) in Lerner, 48.

or Michelangelo's *Pieta*); fear or dread (see Edvard Munch's *The Scream*[31]), loathing or disgust (the art of Serrano and Mapplethorpe). But how can one reasonably call such aesthetic feelings and emotions "enjoyed perception"? We don't "enjoy" them or find them "pleasant" in any way, but they do fascinate and arouse us.

Of course one way of getting around this problem is to make certain distinctions, e.g. between ordinary aesthetic experiences and uniquely aesthetic or artistic ones, or between ordinary emotions and aesthetic emotions. Dewey himself,[32] his many admirers,[33] formalists such as Clive Bell,[34] and others often do this. The problems with such a subterfuge (as a critic might call it) are first, making sense of these quite uncommon distinctions, and second, avoiding what Dewey himself assiduously tried to avoid, namely making art and aesthetic experience something totally divorced from ordinary life and bordering on the occult.

Dewey's own anti-dualism approach in philosophy conflicts with attempts to make such distinctions. If it is all right to make a distinction between aesthetic emotions and non-aesthetic emotions, why isn't it all right to insist on a distinction between art and craft, which Dewey seems to want to deny. But perhaps Dewey's anti-dualism is too extreme a position to take. Let us take a closer look, at the art/craft distinction. Most persons including pragmatists would no doubt grant that every art work is based on craftsmanship, i.e. a knowledge of how to use the appropriate tools, shape the material, etc. An architect couldn't be much of an architect if he or she weren't also a reasonably good draftsman. But one can be the latter without the talent of the former. William James found that he was a reasonably good draughtsman (British spelling used also by Bell and by Wright) but a poor visualizer and so gave up trying to become a professional painter.

---

31 In Norwegian: *Skirk,* perhaps better translated into English as *Shriek,* suggesting prolonged agony. Munch produced four versions of the painting, the fourth of which sold for $119, 922, 600. See Wikipedia entry, *The Scream.*

32 Dewey, *Experience and Nature,* 375-77.

33 Cf. Leddy, *The Extraordinary in the Ordinary,* 59, 61, 63-64, 78-79, 173, who also mentions other aestheticians who make this distinction.

34 See below 76.

Frank Lloyd Wright began his career as a draftsman at a Chicago architectural firm, becoming the "best-paid draughtsman in Chicago," he says,[35] and only later evolved into the greatest architect of his time. The difference between being a craftsman and becoming an artist seems to be that although craft can be reduced to rules and techniques and taught, having the insight, judgment, and talent of the artist is not capable of being taught or learned, despite Dewey's apparent claim otherwise. Even Immanuel Kant maintained that good judgment in practical matters, especially in matters of morality and taste, can not be taught or learned in the usual manner. One either has it or one does not.[36]

Insofar as Dewey's anti-dualism leads him to deny this distinction between art and craft, and correspondingly the distinction between the ordinary and the super ordinary or extraordinary, and requires him to make distinctions between aesthetic emotions and ordinary ones, it is apparent that his views have gone far beyond what the pragmatic perspective requires. It is no wonder that Stephen Pepper came to believe that Dewey had abandoned pragmatism, although, as noted above, for quite other and wrong reasons.

During his lifetime Dewey, because of his forward looking emphasis so typical of pragmatism, was accused of having no place for history in his philosophy, and specifically of having no cognizance of the history of aesthetics. Dewey of course denied the allegations.[37] Indeed, in *Experience and Nature,* chapter 3, entitled "Nature, Ends and Histories," he discusses Greek art and especially what Plato and Aristotle said about it. He even observes that "The Aristotelian conception of four-fold 'causation' is openly

---

35 Wright, *An Autobiography,* 106

36 Cf. Kant *Fundamental Principles of the Metaphysics of Morals*: "This concept [of a goodwill] requires not so much to be taught as merely to be clarified.;" *Critique of Practical Reason*: "Nature seems to have provided us only in a stepmotherly fashion with a faculty needed [to discern our highest good]." 151-52; *Critique of Judgment*: " Only when men have got all they want can we tell who among the crowd has taste or not;" (292, Friedrich); "Theory and Practice": "Since there cannot again be rules for judgment on how a subsumption is to be achieved .. . . there will be theoreticians who, in their whole lives, can never become practical because they lack judgment." 412.

37 Dewey, "Experience, Knowledge and Value: A Rejoinder," in *The Philosophy of John Dewey,* ed. Paul Arthur Schilpp, 515-608.

borrowed from the arts,"[38] a method of analysis adopted in this very book. Also speaking of symbolism (in art and in human culture generally), he says,

> The pervasive operation of symbolism in human culture is all the proof that is needed to show that an intimate and direct sense of place and connection[39] in a prolonged history enters into the enjoyed and suffered constituents of the history, and especially into the final or terminal members.[40]

Or again regarding the role of history in the development of the arts,

> In short, the history of human experience is a history of the development of the arts. The history of science in its distinct emergence from religious, ceremonial, and poetic arts is the record of a differentiation of arts, not a record of separation from art.[41]

But what about contemporary history, in particular about current theories of aesthetics? Admittedly Dewey does not spend much time discussing contemporary theories, but it is not true that he was totally unaware of them. For example, he refers specifically to the theory of "significant form" as a "definition of an esthetic object."[42] This is a clear reference to Clive Bell, although he doesn't actually name him.

Nor are references to history foreign to most writers on pragmatism. O.W. Holmes, Jr. spent years investigating the historical origins of basic legal

---

38   Dewey, *Experience and Nature*, 92.
39   Dewey's use here of the expression "sense of place and connection" corroborates the view that a sense of place is a normative or value-oriented concept and as useful in understanding aesthetics as it is in understanding morality. Cf. Davis: *The Philosophy of Place,* especially Ch. IX, "Poetry and Place" and Ch. X, "The Sense of Place." Also "William James, John Stuart Mill, and a Sense of Place" in Davis: *Comparative Philosophy*, Ch. VI.
40   Dewey, *Experience and Nature,* 387.
41   Ibid., 388.
42   Ibid., 391.

concepts of English common law, later revealed in his book, *The Common Law*. William James was not overly concerned with history except perhaps for the history of pragmatism itself, but it is clear from the many scholarly references in his writings (e.g. to "primitive Christianity" and to Luther & Wesley in "The Sentiment of Rationality;"; to Calvin & Newman in "The Moral Philosopher and the Moral Life"; to the history of medicine and physiology as well as psychology, in his *Principles of Psychology*; also to "primitive literature" in the chapter on Reasoning in PP-II; and to biblical and Jewish history in *The Varieties of Religious Experience*), that he was no stranger to history and had no difficulty incorporating it into his philosophical and psychological writings and theories.

Given all these interests in history by pragmatists, it is clear that Dewey can be absolved from one more false accusation leveled against his theory of aesthetics. Yet the accusation, though false, does raise a related question which Collingwood, another expressionist, discusses at some length, and that is whether art has a history in the same sense that science and philosophy have. Once again let us try to restrict our attention to public art and architecture, since what may be true of it may not be true of art in general.

Collingwood, like Dewey, is convinced that "the aesthetician . . . is not concerned with dateless realities lodged in some metaphysical heaven, but with the facts of his own place and his own time."[43] Speaking specifically of architecture, he then goes on to cite

> [John] Ruskin who . . . insisted long ago that in the special case of architecture the best work demanded a genuine collaboration between designer and executants: not a relation in which the workmen simply carried out orders, but one in which they had a share in the work of designing. Ruskin did not succeed in his project of reviving English architecture, because he only saw his own idea dimly and could

43 R.G. Collingwood, *The Principles of Art*, 325. This statement clearly and unequivocally indicates that he too believes in the relevance and importance of the concept of place in aesthetics, as Clive Bell does not. Cf. *Art*, 34.

not think out its implications, which was done better by William Morris; but the idea he partly grasped is one application of the idea I shall try to state.[44]

The idea, or "application of the idea," he enunciates is one which Dewey develops in much greater detail (almost *ad nauseum*), namely that the artist's act must be coupled or blended with some act of receptive appreciation by the consumer/observer. In music this blending occurs, Collingwood suggests, when the score of the composer is sprinkled with "expression marks" for the executants (the musicians); or in drama the behavior described by the playwright is modified by the interpretative behavior of the performers. As he summarizes it, "We must face the fact that every performer is of necessity a co-author." This mingling or blending may be far more pronounced in architecture than in the other arts, but still he maintains very pragmatically that "Art is not contemplation, it is action."[45]

In his book, *The Idea of History*, Collingwood expresses the rather startling view that art so conceived has no history. Art, he claims, involves a process of converting "unreflective to reflective thought" and that is not something which can be re-enacted and so made a matter of record for history. There can, he says, be a history of art (or artifacts), i.e. the physical objects of aesthetic experience, but there can be "no history of artistic problems as there is a history of scientific or philosophical problems."[46]

He claims that in science and philosophy the situation is different.

> An intelligent [historical] inquiry into the influence of Socrates on Plato, or Descartes on Newton, seeks to discover not the points of agreement, but the way in which the

---

44 Ibid., 326-27.
45 Ibid., 332.
46 Collingwood, *The Idea of History*, 314.

conclusions reached by one thinker give rise to problems for the next.

The artist, unlike the scientist, does not start out with a problem such as discovering the cause of a disease, and by reviewing and incorporating others' contributions to the solution proceed to solve it.[47] The artist, Collingwood contends, "does not appear to set out on a particular piece of work with a clearly formulated problem . . . He seems to be working in a world of pure imagination . . . never in any sense knowing what he is going to do until he has done it."[48] There is no way the historian can insert him or herself into the mind of a creative artist such as Michelangelo at this stage, as the historian can re-enact the thought of a scientist such as Newton or a philosopher such as Descartes. Thus, in accordance with Collingwood's theory of re-enactment (i.e., the literal identification of historian's mind with that of the historical figure), there can be no history of art as properly understood.

Yet if art *is* action, as he definitely says it is, one can't help wondering why these acts or actions of the artists aren't just as recordable as those of the scientist or the philosopher. One can, and many have, reasonably questioned Collingwood's theory of history which gives rise to this theory of artistic re-enactment. Since that is not our concern here, we shall pass no judgment upon it, but observe only that neither Dewey nor any other pragmatists have adopted it.[49]

---

47 In this respect, Collingwood agrees with Bell who said, "To think of a man's art as leading on to the art of someone else is to misunderstand it." *Art,* 75.

48 Collingwood, *The Idea of History,* 313.

49 Dewey would certainly object to Collingwood's suggestion that the artist, unlike the scientist and the philosopher, does not start out from what Dewey calls a "problematic situation."

Chapter VIII

IS SENTIMENTALITY THE GANGRENE OF PUBLIC ART AND ARCHITECTURE? ARE ILLUSTRATIONS OF ORDINARY LIFE ART?

The *Jefferson Memorial* in Washington, D. C. is reported to have been called "a gangrene of sentimentality" by no less an architect than Frank Lloyd Wright.[1] It is hardly necessary here and now to rehearse all the extensive controversy surrounding its location, design, and construction (1939-1943). Suffice it to say that it was pushed from start to finish by President Franklin Delano Roosevelt, a profound admirer of Jefferson, and is now ranked by the American Institute of Architects as fourth on its list of America's most favorite examples of architecture. However, the accusation that the Memorial suffers from sentimentality provokes the question, What's so sickly sentimental about it? And is this a "gangrene" which infects, or can infect, all public art and architecture?

The major criticisms of the Memorial at the time of its completion were largely based on its neo-classical design. The Columbia University School of Architecture condemned it as "a lamentable misfit in time and place," The League for Progress in Architecture objected to the Memorial as "serving no purpose whatsoever," and Frank Lloyd Wright in a letter to Franklin

---

1 Cf. Sandra Beasley, "American Idol," *The Washington Post Magazine,* Nov. 15, 2009, 24. Also, Davis, *The Philosophy of Place,* 5, 130-31.

D. Roosevelt, in addition to regarding it as "a gangrene of sentimentality," called it "an arrogant insult to the memory of Thomas Jefferson."[2]

Roosevelt himself was immune to these criticisms. He himself approved the design, which he had insisted be compatible with the other neo-classical monuments in Washington, such as the Supreme Court Building, the National Gallery, the National Archives, et al. He had some reservations regarding the estimated cost of $10 million and wanted it reduced to $3 million, which Congress subsequently appropriated, but otherwise he was quite satisfied with the project designed by John Russell Pope, which incorporates certain Jeffersonian features such as a domed ceiling and Doric columns like those at Monticello and the Rotunda at the University of Virginia. The interior bronze statue of Jefferson was sculpted by Rudulph Evans. It's installation was delayed until 1947, four years after the 1943 dedication of the Memorial itself, because of the WWII demands for money and materials.

Some critics objected to the classical style on the ground that Hitler and the Nazis had also adopted grandiose versions of Roman and Greek architecture to highlight their totalitarian regime. Roosevelt was not swayed. He adamantly maintained that the Memorial would stand as an affirmation of freedom, an example of great art, and a determination that our nation should not perish from the earth, no matter how our enemies seek to destroy us.

One can, and many at the time did, argue about the appropriateness of the Memorial, its classical design, its setting, its meager subsidy, but all those considerations now seem antiquated. Yet Wright's comment about sentimentality, and that of others as well about sentimentalism in art, remains. We have already encountered another instance of alleged sentimentality in or associated with great art, namely, William James' story of the English couple who while gazing at Titian's painting, "Assumption," uttered such comments as "What a *deprecatory* expression her face wears!" "What self *abnegation*!" "How *unworthy* she feels of the honor she is receiving!"

<hr />

2 See "Classical America," Remarks by William J. van den Heuvel, at the presentation of the Arthur Ross Awards, The National Academy of Design, May 1, 2000.

James' comment: "Their honest hearts had been kept warm all the time by a glow of spurious sentiment that would have fairly made old Titian sick." (PP-II, 472). Dewey calls attention to this passage in James' *Psychology* for a somewhat different purpose, i.e., to describe the character of a consummatory experience, but there is good reason to suppose that he like James and James' father (though perhaps not his brother Henry) would also be sickened by such "spurious" sentimentality.

But before inquiring more deeply into what both Wright and James might have meant by that expression, or by sentimentalism in general, let us consider another artist whose work has been denigrated by many critics as mere illustration, or as Clive Bell might negatively have described it, as "descriptive art," whose sole aim is the sentimental portrayal of ordinary American life. Some have used the expressions "bourgeois," "kitsch," "sweet," "whimsical," "banal," and "non-serious" to describe Norman Rockwell's work. Incidentally, Rockwell himself never objected to being called an illustrator, because that is what he called himself. However, that was perhaps only an act of modesty; he may simply have regarded the term "artist" an honorific title to be bestowed only on those of superior talent, just as many a professor of philosophy shies away from being called a philosopher, because loving philosophy above all other disciplines, he regards it as an honorific title.

The Rockwell case, however, presents us with a complex problem, in fact with two extremely difficult problems. First, although it can hardly be denied that many of his illustrations for *The Saturday Evening Post, Boys' Life, Coca Cola* advertisements, and other publications were sentimental in the usual sense of that term, and for the most part intended to entertain and amuse, many of his later work such as *The Four Freedoms* concerned with the freedoms mentioned in one of FDR's speeches; his *The Problem We All Live With,* depicting a young black child on her way to school in defiance of segregation; and others dealing with religion, such as the Boy Scout law, *A Scout is Reverent* are depictions of a more serious and less amusing or entertaining character. None of the latter seem to be "sentimental" in the usual sense. Are there in fact many different meanings of the term "sentimental"? Are there good sentiments as well as bad ones as far as art is concerned? As we shall see, these ambiguities affect the ways Wright and James use the expression.

The other major problem Rockwell confronts us with is the challenge it presents to our attempt to deal only with public art rather than with art in general and non-public art in particular. If Rockwell's illustrations are genuinely art, and multitudes would claim that they are, then is it to be classed as public or non-public art? So far in our analysis we have classed paintings and drawings as non-public, although there are some notable exceptions, e.g., Picasso's *Guernica*, which seems aimed at public opinion, and meant to incite action against a vicious, belligerent, and totalitarian regime. The line between public and non-public, as we have seen, is difficult to draw in exact terms, but it does seem to exist and adds clarity to discussions of aesthetics if we make the effort.

Rockwell's work certainly meets some of the criteria. Published mainly in popular magazines, it is clearly aimed at the public; much of it serves social purposes, which hardly need to be spelled out here, and besides being entertaining is interesting in itself. It deals with objects with regard to which one could easily have what Dewey calls a "consummatory experience." The original of *The Problem We All Live With* was displayed in 2011 at the White House during the subject's meeting with President Obama, when she was then an adult of 56 years. His works hang in numerous museums across the country including the Guggenheim. In 2008 Rockwell was designated the official state artist of the Commonwealth of Massachusetts. The Norman Rockwell Museum in Stockbridge, Massachusetts, contains some 700 original paintings, drawings, and studies.

His work is arguably as entitled to the label "public art," as is Picasso's *Guernica*. Yet his work exudes "sentiment" and seemingly of two varieties. Are we then to say that there are two (or more?) kinds of sentiment, and correspondingly, two or more kinds of sentimentality? To answer those questions let us return to Frank Lloyd Wright. If one examines his book *An Autobiography*, one finds that he uses the term sometimes derogatorily and sometimes quite otherwise. For example, discussing his lineage from his mother's family, the Lloyd-Joneses, he describes himself as "The

sentimental son of a sentimental mother grown up in the midst of a sentimental family planted on free soil by a grandly sentimental grandfather . . .
the Welsh pioneer." (60) If being sentimental was such an awful thing, why
would he so lovingly describe his relation to that branch of his family? Why
would he also later change his given middle name from Lincoln to Lloyd,
if he did not fondly regard and feel a certain loyalty to his Welsh ancestor?

Yet Wright also speaks of "sheer ordinary sentimentality," (89) and "in-
sidious sentimentality." (103). Later, however, in what may in fact be an
imaginary conversation with an editor, he discusses "true form" and his
vision for democracy:

> Millions of consciences like yours and mine, likewise
> uneasy, struggling against what seems so unnecessarily
> stupid, so utterly inferior, are essential to the life of any
> honest country wherein Democracy may be after all, only
> that "state of unhappy consciousness," which Hegel said it
> was. . . .

> I know, with good enough reason now, there are many
> loving it just the way I love it: a love that means eventu-
> ally, if not soon, a true democratic Form not only for our
> buildings, but for the appropriate lives we will live in them,
> and even the cultivation of the ground on which they shall
> stand. (381)

Wright in these passages is clearly declaring his love not only for a true
form of democracy but also for a true form for buildings and for human
lives.[3] If that is not a sentiment, and his utterance not an expression of sentimentality, then what should we call it? A word or two about his reference
to Hegel's concept of "an unhappy consciousness" may clarify his meaning.
In his *Phenomenology of Mind,* Hegel spends a lengthy section discussing
the state of mind he calls an "Unhappy Consciousness" (Ger: *Unglückliches*

---

3 By "true form" Wright does not mean anything like what Bell means by "pure form," as we
shall see in greater detail in Ch. IX.

Bewusstsein). William James, who was perhaps influenced by Hegel in this regard, also has a chapter in his *Varieties of Religious Experience* in which he too describes a similar state of mind which he dubs a "Sick Soul." In both cases they are speaking of a mind or person who takes life seriously, bordering on pessimism, but who nonetheless is strong enough not to succumb to the pressures of life and intelligent enough to find ways of combating evil. James contrasts this kind of person or mind with what he calls a "Healthy-Minded Soul," a born optimist who, however, fails in the face of danger and reality. According to James the "Sick Soul" will always win over the "Healthy-Minded Soul."

If this view that the Unhappy Consciousness or Sick Soul is superior to the Cheerful Consciousness or Healthy-minded Soul is indeed maintained not only by Wright but also by James and Hegel (who incidentally also said that nothing great was ever accomplished without passion[4]), then how does it apply to Wright's negative appraisal of the Jefferson Memorial. By calling it a "gangrene of sentimentality," Wright may have meant that it evoked only the sentiments of the Healthy-minded, and was out of touch with things as they were in Jefferson's day and in our own. Since Jefferson, in his opinion, was more like the Unhappy Consciousness and more intelligent than the average person in assessing things as they really were, the monument was, he thought, an "arrogant insult" to his memory.

Yet what is there about the Memorial which could bring Wright to such a conclusion? Surely it can't be simply because Wright himself disdained classical architecture, curved domes, or Doric columns, or because it houses a bronze statue of Jefferson. Frankly, it boggles the mind. Perhaps the only aspect of the structure which might reasonably have offended Wright is the fact, which many historians and Jefferson scholars have discovered, that many of the quotations of Jefferson's words inscribed on the interior walls are inaccurate. Statements from the *Declaration of Independence* have been altered; references to the right of revolution omitted; others misleadingly truncated or shortened to save space. Like Jefferson himself, Wright

---

4 Hegel, *Lectures on the Philosophy of History,* 374,

aimed in his architecture to get things right, and these errors may have seemed to him like stains on TJ's memory.

It seems also relevant here to point out that William James too has at times referred to sentiments and sentimentality in two quite different and incompatible senses. On the one hand, he excoriates the excessive emotionalism of the English couple viewing Titian's portrait, but he also, as we have previously observed,[5] maintains that there are two orders of things, the mechanical and the sentimental. He also wrote an article entitled "The Sentiment of Rationality," which provides a view of sentimentality and rationality which is considerably different from traditional ways of viewing them. Understanding these latter distinctions depends somewhat on determining whether or not and to what extent art (public or otherwise) is meant to be informative, descriptive (a term Bell uses in a derogatory sense) or otherwise representative of reality. It seems appropriate, therefore, to postpone discussion of them until these questions have been dealt with.

---

5 Cf. below, 22.

Chapter IX

IS PUBLIC ART REPRESENTATIONALISM AT ITS WORST?
ARE ARTISTS PROFESSIONAL LIARS?
IS ART THE ANTITHESIS OF KNOWLEDGE?
CAN OBJECTIVE JUDGMENTS ABOUT ART BE MADE?

Unless one adopts the rather sophomoric conception of art as a kind of amusement which affords us pleasure— which much great or even just good art often does not—it is perfectly natural, understandable, and legitimate to suppose that art will at least tell us something we didn't otherwise know. Yet this view seems to commit us to the notion that art in this respect is like science, history, philosophy, sociology or some other intellectual discipline which aims at discovering truth about the world we inhabit.[1] We get the idea that just as the scientist seeks a *correspondence* or some kind of *agreement* between what's in his or her mind (e.g., images, ideas, theories, etc.) and what's out there in our physical, psychological, and social worlds,[2] so the artist in a similar fashion seeks to provide a *representation*, *imitation*, or *copy* of those realities, or their emotional effects upon

---

1 Or in the case of poetry as John Haines puts it, "something that comes close to what we understand as 'truth,'" and not "truth in a narrow sense." *Living Off the Country: Essays on Poetry and Place,* 3, quoted in Davis, *The Philosophy of Place, 2-3, 112.*

2 James, in "Pragmatism's Conception of Truth," says, "Pragmatists and intellectualists both accept this definition as a matter of course. They begin to quarrel only after the question is raised as to what may precisely be meant by the term "agreement," and what by the term "reality," when reality is taken as something for our ideas to agree with." 198

us, by means of their art works, whether they be paintings, sculptures, music, dramas, buildings, bridges, wind farms, musical water fountains, dances, or parades. Unfortunately, although this view is to a degree very commonsensical, it can lead a person who is not in tune with his feelings, or as Clive Bell puts it, "has no faculty for distinguishing a work of art from a handsaw,"[3] to think, for example, that a painting or portrait is little different from a photograph and proceeds to judge its artistic quality by determining how accurately the painting copies or is "like" the art subject. To such a person the work of art is either a good "likeness" or it is not. But such a conception of art is both absurd and futile. It is absurd because if all the artist intends is the production of an exact copy, then he would achieve that end much better, not by using paints and canvas, but modern photographic and other kinds of reproductive devices and materials. From the observer or art consumer point of view such an attempt to evaluate the art would amount to a futile effort since no determination of the exactness of the copy could be made unless the subject were still alive and available for inspection. Even then time would have elapsed and changes in the subject occurred, and so any such comparison would necessarily involve a departure from the original situation.

But if it is naïve to suppose that art is merely imitative or a copy of reality, is it then only a projection of the artist's imagination? And if we take it as "true of" something (or put otherwise "tells us something") is that nothing but a kind of lie, and the artist nothing more than a professional liar? Both Collingwood and Bell raise this issue,[4] and both raise serious objections to it based on their own distinctive theories, the details of which we need not get into here. It is pertinent to note, however, that this notion that art is in some sense a falsification (whether deliberate as in the case of a lie, or mistaken due to a lack of talent or insight) can be traced all the way back to Plato. His view went something like the following. Take any building, whether the Jefferson Memorial, the Lincoln Memorial, the National Gallery, or the Supreme Court Building—its ultimate reality

---

3 Bell, *Art*, 15.
4 Bell, *Art*, 18-19, 48-49; Collingwood, *The Principles of Art*, 219, 286.

resides in an ideal building existing in a sort of "metaphysical heaven" (to use Collingwood's term) and is usually referred to by the word *Idea* or *Form* [in Greek, *Eidos*]. The empirical version of this Form is the one we are immediately acquainted with through the senses. The artist's depiction is of this empirical version and so, from a metaphysical point of view, is twice removed from the ultimate reality, and consequently and inevitably a distortion of it. Plato uses this theory of Forms to make his case that therefore art is inherently and fundamentally antithetical to truth and knowledge.

If the pragmatist, along with Bell and Collingwood, wishes to reject the Platonic position as well as the copy theory, what then is, or should be, the pragmatist's position regarding representationalism in the arts? William James cautions that the pragmatist, first of all, must refrain from committing what he calls the "sentimentalist fallacy" which involves extracting "a quality from the muddy particulars of experience" and finding "it so pure when extracted that they contrast it with each and all its muddy instances as . . . opposite. . . in nature...."[5] His description fits very nicely the viewpoint of an aesthetician such as Clive Bell who thinks of art as involving the abstraction of a "pure" or "significant form" from ordinary (in James' language "muddy") experience. A. N. Whitehead is similarly wary of the same fault but calls it the "fallacy of misplaced concreteness," which he defines as "mistaking. . . abstraction[s] for concrete realities." [6] Immanuel Kant, by implication at least, suggests the fallacy involves a "misapplication of theory to practice" which occurs, for example, when a theoretician, although knowledgeable but lacking good judgment, attempts to give practical advice. As he explains, "There are doctors and lawyers who, although they did well in school, do not know what to do when they are called upon to give counsel.[7]

---

5 James, op. cit., 174.

6 Whitehead, *Science and the Modern World*, 55. See also *Process and Reality*, 11.

7 Cf. Kant, "Theory and Practice: Concerning the Common Saying This May Be True in Theory but Does Not Apply to Practice": in *The Philosophy of Kant: Immanuel Kant's Moral and Political Writings*, 412.

One example Whitehead gives of the fallacy of misplaced concreteness, or mistaking abstractions for concrete realities, is when the philosophers and scientists of the seventeenth century took the distinction between primary and secondary qualities in an absolute metaphysical sense, and ended up with a conception of Nature as "a dull affair, soundless, scentless, colorless; merely the hurrying of material, endlessly, meaninglessly."[8]

Perhaps James expresses the fallacy best, although he uses the notoriously ambiguous term "sentimental" to describe it, when he says,

> The "sentimentalist fallacy" is to shed tears over abstract justice and generosity, beauty, etc., and never to know these qualities when you meet them in the street, because the circumstances make them vulgar. Thus I read in the privately printed biography of an eminently rationalistic mind: "It was strange that with such admiration for beauty in the abstract, my brother had no enthusiasm for fine architecture, for beautiful painting, or for flowers.[9]

To assess more positively whether the pragmatic perspective in art includes representation, let us again return to the supposed parallel between the "agreement" in science which is called "truth," and the "representation" in art which one may call "beauty," or if that expression is unacceptable because too overloaded with meanings, perhaps the term "rightness" is appropriate. In epistemology the pragmatist rejects any "static" conception of the relationship between our ideas and their counterparts in reality. Truth cannot be a simple unalterable correspondence between ideas and things. It must entail some process. As James puts it,

> To "agree" in the widest sense with a reality can only mean to be guided either straight up to it or into its surroundings, or to be put into such working touch with it as to

8 Whitehead, *Science and the Modern World*, 56.
9 James, "Pragmatism's Conception of Truth," 173.

handle either it or something connected with it better than if we disagreed.[10]

This view does not totally reject the representation of the one with the other, but he says,

> To copy a reality is, indeed, one very important way of agreeing with it, but it is far from being essential. The essential thing is the process of being guided.[11]

If we turn to the parallel situation in art, the pragmatist again would reject any static relationship between the artistic conscience or temperament (if we may use those terms here) and the contemplated art object, e.g., the proposed prairie style house, or the imagined marble figure of David. As Dewey put it, art is "an active productive process, an esthetic perception," which includes certain "operative efficiencies" and "moving tendencies." Even Collingwood, who shares certain aspects of what we have called the pragmatic perspective, says that "a work of art is an activity of a certain kind."[12] Thus if all one could say of a given work of art was that it had a static relation of correspondence to, or was representative of, or a copy of a certain feature of reality, and in no respects an incitement to action, then all these philosophers would have to agree with Frank Lloyd Wright that it was but a gangrene of sentimentality and an arrogant misunderstanding of the nature of art.

But can we spell out in somewhat greater detail what thinking of art as a kind of activity really entails and how it differs from viewing art statically or as a mere "copy" of reality. Consider a person viewing Michelangelo's David long enough to have a consummatory experience in Dewey's sense. If that person can only wonder why his hands are so large and out of proportion to the rest of his body, or the size or angle of his head exaggerated, or why the figure is uncircumcised and thus inconsistent with Hebrew

---

10   Ibid. 166.
11   Ibid.
12   Collingwood, *The Principles of Art*, 280.

culture, and is a person who has no knowledge of biblical history or the political power of the Medici family in Florence during Michelangelo's time, nor is in any way motivated by the statue to confront tyranny whenever it arises, then from the pragmatist perspective, he or she is indeed like Bell's deaf person at a concert, and the statue is for that person, strictly speaking, non-art, essentially no different from a lump of clay.

But contrary to another aspect of Bell's view, the pragmatist must always remember that art is concerned with the facts of human experience, with this world and not with some world "with an intense and peculiar significance of its own."[13] As Collingwood expresses it, "the aesthetician . . . is not concerned with dateless realities in some metaphysical heaven, but with the facts of his own place and his own time."[14] If that is the case, then we are confronted with a quagmire of problems relating to meaning and truth in the arts. If the arts (including architecture) have meaning, then in some sense they must be descriptive, symbolic, or representative; and so it must be possible for art to express truths about the world, or at least "something like truth," as the poet Haines has said.[15] Whole books have been devoted to just these issues.[16] It would easy to get bogged down in a discussion of them. We have tried to avoid that calamity by restricting our attention to public art rather than to art in general, and indeed we have already broached the subject of artistic meaning in our discussion of Jefferson's Monticello,[17] so it seems unnecessary to review those notions here. However, we have barely touched on the question of truth in the arts, and perhaps a few words might be helpful in explaining the pragmatist's position on this matter.

Actually Collingwood's discussion of this problem in Chapter XIII of his *The Principles of Art* is far superior to and clearer than other accounts, including Dewey's, and although it is in some respects different from what

---

13 Bell, see below 76.
14 Collingwood, below 91.
15 Haines, below, 103, n. 1.
16 See John Hospers, *Meaning and Truth in the Arts,*
17 See below 18.

James has to say (as will be pointed out), it is generally consistent with what we have called the pragmatist perspective. According to Collingwood,

> If what an artist says [i.e., expresses in artistic form] on a given occasion . . . is an act of consciousness . . . it follows that this utterance [or expression], so far from being indifferent to the distinction between truth and falsehood, is necessarily an attempt to state the truth. So far as the utterance is a good work of art, it is a true utterance; its artistic merit and its truth are the same thing.[18]

Collingwood admits that this claim has often been denied but that is because the critics have failed to distinguish two forms of thought, that of intellect which aims at "relational truths" by means of argument, and that of consciousness which does not seek truth by argument or inference but by an immediate apprehension of what he calls "individual facts." Of course if one thinks that intellectual or relational thought which employs argument is the only kind of thought there is, and if conscious artistic expression does not use argument, then it can't be concerned with truth.[19] However, to Collingwood and pragmatist aestheticians generally that is a mistaken and purely dogmatic view.

Collingwood's distinction between intellect and consciousness is more or less the same distinction which James makes when he speaks of two "orders" of reality, namely the *mechanical* order which he associates with analysts who employ "mediational' thought, and the *sentimental* order which he associates with men of intuition.[20] James is as fully appreciative as is Collingwood of the role which intuition of this type plays in the search for knowledge. Later in our examination of his theory of the interrelation of aesthetic, scientific, and moral principles, we shall take account of this in greater detail.

---

18 *The Principles of Art,* 287.
19 Ibid., 287.
20 Cf. below 26.

Collingwood neatly summarizes the position which he, James, Dewey, and other pragmatists hold with regard to the alleged antithesis between art and knowledge as follows:

> Art is not indifferent to truth; it is essentially the pursuit of truth. But the truth it pursues is not a truth of relation, it is a truth of individual fact.[21] . . . Art is knowledge, knowledge of the individual.[22]

As far back as Aristotle, knowledge has rather consistently been understood as knowledge of the universal, not knowledge of the particular, so to say that art is intuitive knowledge of the individual is rather extraordinary. Applying Aristotle's view to painting rather than as he did to drama,[23] consider one of Collingwood's examples. A patron buys a picture of a fox-hunt or a covey of partridges, not because it is a picture of a particular fox-hunt or covey, but because it represents a thing of that kind, what Aristotle would call the "universal" fox-hunt or covey.[24] Understood in this manner the picture provides no knowledge of the individual as such. If then true art is not to be regarded in accordance with the Aristotelian model, then what is it supposed to be representative or "true of"? The best Collingwood can come up with is that it must be representative of the *feelings* which the artist had in creating the art, not the features of the object itself or its "universal" character. Unfortunately putting it this way suggests that art is merely a way of expressing or recollecting emotion. James does not commit himself to such a position and Dewey, as we have already observed explicitly rejects it.[25]

---

21 Collingwood, *The Principles of Art*, 288.
22 Ibid., 289.
23 Aristotle, *Poetics*, 1451a., where he says that "poetry [including drama] is more philosophic and of graver import than history since its statements are of the nature of universals, whereas those of history are singulars."
24 Recall too that John Haines said that besides seeking truth or something like the truth in poetry, it must also be a kind of *universal* truth. Cf. below, 103, n. 1.
25 Cf. Dewey, above, 98; *Experience and Nature*, 390.

So what is, or should be the content of a knowledge of the individual as far as art is concerned. Henry James, Sr. suggests that art should be "the gush of God's life into every form of spontaneous speech and act."[26] Clive Bell is almost as effusive when he suggests

> Instead of recognizing its [the art object's] accidental and conditioned importance, we become aware of its essential reality, of the God in everything, of the universal in the particular, of the all-pervading rhythm.

> Call it by what name you will, the thing that I am talking about is that which lies behind the appearance of all things—that which gives to all things their individual significance . . .[27]

It is perhaps needless to say that pragmatists such as James and Dewey do not endorse such theological and metaphysical views in their theories of art. Instead, they offer a much more practical solution to the problem. Truth in the arts is not obtained by simply copying reality, nor even by a "generalized representation" [28] of it, nor by a kind of "emotional representation," which seems to be Collingwood's view. Rather, the consistent pragmatist must take James at his word when he insists that the good art object "leads" us, that we are "guided" by the work, and are not distracted by making the mistake of confusing the abstract for the concrete or otherwise attempting to explain by theory what can only be grasped by an intimate acquaintance with "muddy" experience. Essentially he is referring to the same components of art and the aesthetic experience which Dewey

---

26 Below, 20.

27 Bell, *Art,* Ch. 3, "The Metaphysical Hypothesis," 54.

28 Collingwood's term for the attempt to grasp the universal aspect of the art object. One must keep in mind, however, that pragmatists do not object to copying reality as such. James says that it is one way to understand or "agree" with it, but not the "essential" way. Nor do pragmatists deny that there can be generalized representations of the Aristotelian type, but object only to attempts to account for the truth in art by substituting an abstraction for a concrete fact. The latter, they maintain, is obtained in art only by viewing art as an activity of a certain type.

stresses when he speaks of "operative efficiencies" and "moving tendencies." Thus truth in art, according to the pragmatic perspective, is what "works" (James' term) or alternatively, is "efficient" in bringing about a certain kind of satisfaction or what Dewey would describe as a "consummatory experience" leading the observer, or art consumer, to the resolution of a problematic situation.

Given this "dynamic," as opposed to the traditional "static" conception of truth, how does the pragmatist account for artistic criticism, i.e. with disagreements with respect to the relative merits of good versus bad art? Since aesthetic judgments on the pragmatist's theory are not propositional, nor arrived at by argument, one cannot contrast them as contradictories. Since they are arrived at by intuition or some kind of immediate awareness, what do we call it when we judge the same art object (building, statue or whatever) differently? My intuition may differ totally from yours, as one activity may differ from another, but if they cannot be thought contradictory in the strict logical sense, then how do we characterize their conflict? And does it make sense to say that one is the "true" activity and the other a "false" activity?

One might say, as an emotional representationalist (or representational emotivist) such as Collingwood does, that the activity judged "bad" is the result of a "corrupt consciousness,"[29] in a person who has had a deficient artistic education or a defect in his or her intuitive abilities. Indeed as we have previously indicated, and as many philosophers of art such as Kant have asserted, many persons simply lack the capacity for good judgment. That of course does not mean that such persons (who often admit that "they don't know much about art, but they know what they like," or who "don't know how to define pornography, but they know it when they see it") refrain from expressing their opinions about it. They continue to make "bad" or "inaccurate" aesthetic judgments all the time.

However, this explanation of the disparity between aesthetic judgments, and art criticism generally, does not seem to be the one pragmatists

---

29 Collingwood, *The Principles of Art*, 117, 119.

accept. In the first place they are more specific about how certain persons, including so-called experts, acquire corrupt artistic consciousnesses. They all seem to agree that such persons frequently commit the fallacy of attempting to substitute abstractions for concrete realities, and also the mistake of supposing that the ultimate subject matter of art is other-worldly, rather than what James rather dramatically refers to as ordinary, "muddy" human experience. Indeed in this connection James gives a quotation from Marcus Aurelius in a lengthy footnote in PP-II, 674-75, which is very revealing of what he has in mind.

> "When we have meat before us, we must receive the impression that this is the dead body of a fish, and this is the dead body of a bird, or of a pig; and again, . . . this purple robe some sheep's wool dyed with the blood of a shell-fish. Such, then, are these impressions, and they reach the things themselves and penetrate them, and we see what kind of things they are. Just in the same way ought we to act through life, and where there are things which appear most worthy of our approbation, we ought to lay them bare and look at their worthlessness and strip them of all the words by which they are exalted."

James, in this context, says,

> Life is one long struggle between conclusions based on abstract ways of conceiving cases, and opposite conclusions prompted by our instinctive perception of them as individual facts. The logical stickler for justice always seems pedantic and mechanical to the man who goes by tact and the particular instance, and who usually makes a poor show at argument.[30]

---

30 James, PP-II, 674, note.

Although he does not advocate seeing the world "in a frosty light from which all fuliginous[31] mists of affection and swamp-lights of sentimentality are absent," James rejects treating "certain concretes by the mere law of their genus. . ."[32] by which he seems to mean treating concrete realities as though they were abstractions.

James believes, however, as do all pragmatists, that the world is rational, i.e., is capable of being understood or known, and that the mind has a certain native structure such that by certain methods of analysis (primarily subsumption and comparison) it can reveal basic relationships in addition to juxtaposition in space and time, which exist within the world. He also believes, as apparently others do not, that there are two kinds of rationality or ways of perceiving relationships, the kind we attribute to science and the other to art. We have been more successful in establishing objective relationships in nature by means of science than we have in art. That is the situation which presently exists he says, "as of now." So far principles in art, which he calls "postulates," are applicable only to *entia rationis,* i.e., to terms in the mind and are not propositions in the same sense that scientific principles are propositions. As a consequence, we find that differing aesthetic judgments may not be rationally conflicting. If one finds Bauhaus architecture beautiful and another finds it cold and uninviting, there is no contradiction. Both opinions and preferences may be rationally well founded, but reason in this case is not reason as employed in science. It is a certain way of grasping the object in its pristine and uniquely individual state, not as glamorized, as Marcus Aurelius would put it, by "exalted" (meaning, "euphemistic") verbiage.

Can there not be legitimate and objective disagreement regarding the merit of a piece of art or architecture? Of course there can be, but resolution of it cannot be by certain tests of validity such as exist in logic and science, since "as of now" they don't exist in aesthetics. Perhaps the best that can be done is to examine the judgmental talents (or lack thereof) in the observers or critics, and the extent of their acquaintance with art objects.

---

31 Meaning "sooty" or "colored by or as if by soot." Cf. *The American Heritage Dictionary.*
32 Ibid., 674.

Most pragmatically oriented philosophers of art would say, in one way or another, that in order for a judgment of the aesthetic quality of a piece of art to "count,"[33] i.e., provide the truth about objective reality, it has to "result in insight, or in an enjoyed perception,"[34] or as Collingwood says, it must involve a mental reconstruction of a "collaboration" between the artist, the audience, and in some cases, the performers of the of the art.[35] James shares these views but because he regards aesthetic judgments as being only about *entia rationis,* he regards them only as "subjective facts."

> They stand waiting in the mind forming a beautiful ideal network; and the most we can say is that we *hope* to discover realities over which the network may be flung so that ideal and real may coincide. [36]

33 Cf. Dewey's use of this term in *Art as Experience,* 354.
34 Ibid.
35 Collingwood, *The Principles of Art,* 141, 251-269, 312, 320-24, 328.
36 James *The Principles of Psychology,* II, 665.

Chapter X

ARE PLACE & COMMUNITY ESSENTIAL INGREDIENTS OF PUBLIC ART? DO PRINCIPLES OF ARTISTIC CREATION STIFLE INNOVATION? CAN THEY BE DISPENSED WITH? JEFFERSON'S, WRIGHT'S, & SPEER'S VIEWS REGARDING THE FORMAL CAUSES OF ART AND ARCHITECTURE

Since public art is by our own definition, and by common understanding, local in character and aimed at the public in general and not specifically at any particular individuals, it is hardly necessary to point out that specific places and identifiable communities are indeed essential components of public art and architecture. However, precisely which places accommodate public art and which communities are regularly and traditionally appealed to still needs to be investigated. A problematic situation exists regarding these matters. To put it bluntly, one does not erect a statue of Hitler in Washington, D.C., nor a statue of Lincoln in the vicinity of Obersalzberg, Austria. Both would be inappropriate and probably, at least in Hitler's day, offensive to the local communities. Even today bitter controversies arise with respect to the placement of public art, whether a monument, a sculpture, or an entire building. The District of Columbia Mall is a favorite site in the United States for patriotic and military memorials, but of course the space available is limited. Aesthetic considerations of symmetry and congruity are often subordinated to political alliances and prejudices. For some unknown reason, there is as of now no statue or other memorial dedicated to John Adams, our second President, anywhere in our national capitol. Although the holocaust of WWII memory now has a museum, it is not on the Mall, nor on one of the avenues bordering it such as Constitution Avenue, but on a mere side street, even though the United States has a Jewish population in the millions, many of whom or their relatives lived through The Holocaust. Currently a memorial to Dwight David Eisenhower, our 34th and much loved President (perhaps one can recall the "I like Ike" badges) is in the planning and execution stage, and yet a great controversy exists regarding where it should be put, and what it should look like.

The communities to which public art is addressed also dictate in rather definite ways the kind of art which is accepted by those communities. For example, no one would think of building an Opera House or a Symphony Hall, such as those in Boston, New York, or Milan, unless the acoustics were designed to project the voices of the singers or the sound of the orchestras, no matter how beautiful the chandeliers. Sculpture or mountain carvings such as those at Mt. Rushmore in South Dakota or outside Atlanta, Georgia, have to be large enough to be viewed and appreciated by persons viewing them from a distance. Japanese gardens, such as the Hakone Garden in Los Gatos, California, are likewise designed to accommodate and stimulate the tactile and olfactory senses. It is rather difficult to imagine an *objet d'art* which functions primarily to excite the taste buds,[1] but perhaps a proper tribute to the culinary genius of Julia Child should include not only her famous television kitchen, which already resides in the Smithsonian Museum, but also the actual taste of her preparations. A hint of that aspect of her artistic achievement is suggested in the DVD, "Julie and Julia," in which her devoted disciple places a pound of butter in the Smithsonian reproduction of her Cambridge, Massachusetts kitchen.

Indeed, community is a vital ingredient of public art, without which music halls, sculptures, gardens, and kitchens would be only places for the deaf, the sightless, and those without a sensitivity to smell, taste,

---

1 A room plastered with beeswax having a food scent has been suggested by one person.

or feeling. An exaggeration? To the contrary, consider how many times one hears complaints about the acoustics of an auditorium, the lack of clarity or precision in a sculpture, how bad the food, or how immune the artist is to natural feelings of revulsion and distaste for pornography. The notion of community, and even "community standards," to use a legal expression, does make sense, if not always, at least to a considerable degree.

Besides being influenced by locations (i.e., places), and those toward whom their art is directed (i.e., communities), public artists (such as architects, sculptors, dramatists, dancers, musicians, bridge builders, parade organizers, and a multitude of others) are also restricted by rules governing their activities. Maybe there are artists who feel they are governed by no such rules, or only by rules of their own making (artistic entrepreneurs such as Christo or Mapplethorpe perhaps), but they are relatively few in number. Most public artists admit to obeying certain basic rules of their arts and crafts, just as professional doctors, lawyers, scientists, and engineers do quite candidly and publicly.

This circumstance is especially true of architects. Their genre, if we may call it that, is deeply infused with what we have called "formal causes." The rules governing architecture have a long history, and although they may have changed over the centuries, some of the most ancient rules still survive. For example, Jefferson was immensely influenced in his architectural ventures by Palladio's *I Quatro Libri dell'Architettura* (The Four Books), which were first published in the 16th century. They, and the architectural principles they contained, were in turn derived in part from those publicized by the ancient Roman architect, Vitruvius. No one seems to know exactly when Vitruvius was born or died, but he "flourished" 46-30 BC. Much of the government architecture in Washington, D. C. today is the product of the thought of just those architects.

That particular thread of history is really quite fascinating, so perhaps a slight digression here is permissible. 'Palladio' is actually a nickname given to an actual individual named at birth, *Andrea di Pietro della Gondola* from Padua, Italy. It was given to him by one Count Giangiorgio Trissino after he became his protégé. The name 'Palladio' is apparently derived from 'Pallas' itself another name for Athena (or Athene), the Greek goddess associated with wisdom and for whom the city of Athens is named.[2]

Vitruvius' full name is *Marcus Vitruvius Pollo*, who has the unique distinction of being the author of the only substantial treatise on antique architecture to have survived that period of enormous architectural activity in ancient Rome and Greece. His book is entitled *De Architectura* and divided into ten "books" or sections, the first five of which were printed in English in 1771 and the entire ten in 1791. Thomas Jefferson is one of the very few in America at that time who knew about Vitruvius and possessed a copy of his book.

Besides reading and studying Vitruvius, Palladio also examined the ruins of ancient culture in Rome itself, and tried to extract many of the designs, styles, and formal causes of those public structures. Since other architects' writings were unfortunately no longer extant, he attempted to reconstruct what may have been their basic notions and rules. What he came up with and subsequently bequeathed to the world has had an immense effect. However, one has to wonder whether some secrets of classical architecture have been as yet undiscovered, and whether what we are left with is only one style, one version of ancient architecture and only one set of aesthetic principles. Has our reliance on those principles, so carefully and skillfully described by Palladio only brought monotony into architecture over the centuries, and in effect stifled innovation?[3]

There can be little doubt that most persons desire, and often demand, a variety of styles and elevations in architecture. A rigid adherence to and repetition of a specific façade or geometric design of a building or of a series of buildings can be extremely dull and uninteresting. Thus "row houses," whether in Baltimore, Dublin, or London, can seem monotonously the same. Painting the doorways with brightly colored and glossy enamel is the way some builders attempt to offset the repetitiveness and platitudinous

---

2 Cf. "Palladio, Andrea," *Oxford Dictionary of Architecture.*
3 It has been alleged that Vitruvius' book "has acquired a [wholly unwarranted] reputation for dullness and obfuscation." Ibid., see "Vitruvius Pollo, Marcus,"

character of these dwellings. Sometimes the result is pleasing, but too often the lack of individuality and innovation shines through.

The same problem with symmetry as a cardinal rule of public art also exists with respect to the construction of whole neighborhoods, clusters of government buildings squeezed into city centers, or the vast diversity of structures erected on college campuses where we find not only classroom buildings, libraries, dormitories, and sporting facilities, but also bookstores, garages, chapels, power plants, and on a few campuses, even barns and horse stables. The founders of such institutions usually aim at producing a certain uniformity in their external appearance, and so again we have another attempt to adhere to the rule of symmetry. Yet unless the college or other institution is small and has relatively few buildings, the growth of such campuses, architecturally speaking, takes off in a multitude of different directions.

At Harvard University, Cambridge, Massachusetts, for example, there are red brick buildings dating back to 1636 when the institution was founded,[4] but also monstrous buildings of a distinctly different Civil War style such as Memorial Hall and Sever Hall, as well as Bauhaus structures such as the Gropius Complex of residence halls, a product of the WWII era. Looked at as a whole rather than at particular sections such as The Yard, the Charles River Houses, or the Business School, each group of which exhibits a certain symmetry and uniformity, the totality of Harvard University architecture represents an appalling jumble[5]. Obviously the Governing Boards over the years have decided that diversity has a certain charm which uniformity lacks, or perhaps have deliberately encouraged differences in the buildings in order to provoke interest, or provide models for art students, particularly those pursuing a career in architecture.

Indeed the latter notion was precisely what Thomas Jefferson had in mind when he designed the "Grounds" of the University of Virginia at Charlottesville. All of the ten pavilions facing the "Lawn" flowing down in

---

4 Actually Massachusetts Hall, built in 1720, is the oldest still-standing red brick building, but the others like it in the Yard are presumably rebuilt structures like the original dormitories, and many still without updated plumbing.

5 An excellent place, however, to study architecture, or at least the history of architecture.

terraces from the Rotunda at the far end (which, incidentally, was meant by Jefferson to be primarily a Library, not a Temple or a Church as was then the custom) have different "orders" of columns, including the Ionic, the Doric, and the Corinthian, and others as well, either of the ancient Greek or Roman styles. The overall effect when viewing this aspect of his design is not, however, one of complete abandonment of a symmetrical style, since all the columns serve to decorate the exteriors of the buildings and support the overhanging porches. Yet if one goes to the trouble to inspect them individually he or she will detect all the differences Jefferson expected serious students to study and become intimately acquainted with.

Something like this architectural practice also occurred at Yale University but to a lesser degree. Many of the dormitories and classroom buildings are constructed, on their exterior sides, strictly in accordance with "Georgian" design, a style developed in England during the reigns of the four King Georges (1714-1830), and influenced by a renewed interest in "Palladianism." The interior sides of these buildings, viewed from their courtyards, are constructed in accordance with a "Gothic" or "Gothic Revival" style. Newer buildings on the Yale campus and in the surrounding neighborhoods of New Haven, Connecticut, have quite different styles, as one might expect since deliberate innovations are now encouraged.

But if such departures from architectural principles of the past are so current, because thought to have a stifling effect on novelty and innovation, then perhaps we can dispense with them, along with all other such "formal causes." Indeed just such an abandonment of principles, at least with respect to ethics and law, has been advocated by a recent pragmatic philosopher, and Yale classmate of mine, Richard Rorty.[6] If his view makes sense, then why may we not adopt a similar abandonment of principle in aesthetics, especially since common architectural practices seem already to have done just that? But let us examine this view more closely to determine whether in fact it is consistent with what we have called the pragmatic perspective.

---

6 Cf. Rorty, "Ethics Without Principles" in his *Philosophy and Social Hope*; also "The Banality of Pragmatism and the Poetry of Justice," in the same volume, particularly note 44.

The disdain which Rorty has for ultimate principles in morals and law seems largely to be based on his contempt for the notion of one single all-pervasive scientific method. Ever since Thomas S. Kuhn pointed out persuasively that science historically has not been as methodical as has been believed,[7] and that there is no such thing as a single Scientific Method, but only many different methods or "vocabularies," as he and other language analysts would prefer to say,[8] the idea of finding and formulating a single unifying principle, whether in science, law, or ethics, has come to be regarded as otiose.

It has also been maintained that it is anti-pragmatic or inconsistent with pragmatism. It is significant that Rorty says for example, that Charles Sanders Peirce's "contribution to pragmatism was merely to have given it a name, and to have stimulated James."[9] The main reason he gives for the "over-praising" of Peirce as the father of modern pragmatism is that "his talk about a general theory of signs looks like an early discovery of the importance of language," but "for all his genius," says Rorty, "Peirce never made up his mind what he wanted a theory of signs *for*, nor what it might look like, nor what its relation to either logic or epistemology was supposed to be."[10] Rorty rejects Peirce's, and all other attempts to ground our culture, our moral lives, our politics, or our religious beliefs upon "philosophical bases," meaning of course alleged unifying principles.

In support of his position, Rorty might also have pointed out that Justice Oliver W. Holmes, a legal pragmatist, early in his career sought to find a set of empirically derived Common Law principles in terms of which all legal problems might be expressed and resolved, and later abandoned the task.[11] Holmes also rejected the Utilitarian principle that one should always seek to promote the greatest good for the greatest number;[12] Kant's principle

---

7 Kuhn, *The Structure of Scientific Revolutions.* See also Rorty, *Consequences of Pragmatism,* 213.

8 Cf. Rorty, "Method, Social Science, and Social Hope," section I, entitled "Science Without Method," in *Consequences of Pragmatism,* 193, 198.

9 Ibid., 161.

10 Ibid.

11 For a fuller discussion of this matter, see Davis, *Comparative Philosophy,* 112-13.

12 Holmes, "*The Gas Stoker's Strike,* 7 ALR 582 (1873). Lerner, 51.

that humans are ends in themselves and never to be treated as means;[13] as well as Hegel's theory of punishment that since a wrong is a negation of a right, punishment should be a negation of that negation and equal to it."[14] Holmes also rejected Spencer's maxim that "a citizen is at liberty to do as he likes so long as he does not interfere with the liberty of others to do the same." [15] However, it must also be pointed out that despite the quarrels Holmes had with all these ethical, legal, and economic principles, he never totally abandoned the notion of having principles in law.[16]

Similarly for James. Although he too rejected the Principle of Utility, essentially for reasons based on psychological considerations,[17] and also attacked other ethical principles such as the survival or self-preservationist principle which he said "fails us when we need it most," he does not abandon his search for an ethical principle which, in his opinion, would not only spell out one's own ideals, but also could accommodate differing viewpoints and "satisfy the alien demands."[18]

The pragmatist, however, who seems to have confronted the precise issue of the role of principles in the normative areas of human conduct head-on rather than tangentially, has been John Dewey. He devotes an entire chapter to "The Nature of Principles" in his *Human Nature and Conduct,* Ch. VII, and makes numerous references to the subject in his *Logic: The Theory of Inquiry.* It is relevant to see what he, as a prominent pragmatist, has to say about it, especially since Rorty claims to be his disciple.[19] Some of his initial comments seem at first to support rule-scepticism. Thus he says,

---

13 Holmes, *The Common Law,* Lecture II.

14 Holmes, Ibid.

15 Holmes, "The Path of the Law," Lerner, 80.

16 For confirmation of this claim, see Davis, *Comparative Philosophy,* Ch. VII, "The Logic of Choice: Holmes on Decisions; James on Beliefs," 112-14.

17 James, "The Moral Philosopher and the Moral Life," in *Essays on Faith and Morals,* 186.

18 James, Ibid., 201, 205. For more on his attempt to find just such a principle, see Davis, *The Philosophy of Place,* Ch. V, "The Ethics of Place," 63.

19 Rorty, *Philosophy and Social Hope,* xvi.

Ready-made rules available at a moment's notice for settling any kind of moral difficulty and resolving every species of moral doubt have been the chief object of the ambition of moralists. . . In morals a hankering for certainty, born of timidity and nourished by a love of authoritative prestige, has led to the idea that absence of immutably fixed and universally applicable ready-made principles is equivalent to moral chaos.[20]

In purely legal matters he also maintains that

Many men are now aware of the harm done . . . by assuming the antecedent existence of fixed principles under which every new case may be brought.[21]

Dewey's own view, however, is a theory of rule-governance, although he advises against thinking of rules and principles as immutably fixed. That latter position, he suggests, only makes situations more complex. They should be viewed as experimental hypotheses, as helpful methods of inquiry, empirical generalizations, or, as he also says, "instrumentalities for the investigation of doubtful cases."

It is clear that all principles are empirical generalizations from the ways in which previous judgments of conduct have practically worked out. When this fact is apparent, these generalizations will be seen to be not fixed rules for deciding doubtful cases, but instrumentalities for their investigation, methods by which thenet value of past experience is rendered available for present scrutiny of new perplexities. then it will also follow that they

---

20   Dewey, *Human Nature and Conduct,* 238.
21   Ibid., 239.

are hypotheses to be tested and revised by their further working.[22]

Far from rejecting principles, it is patently clear that Dewey wholeheartedly accepts them, and indeed, when seen in the way he has described them, cautions that

Lightly to disregard them is the height of foolishness![23]

In aesthetics, Dewey explicitly rejects pure formalism, as he also does even in logic and mathematics [which fortunately we need not have to try to explicate here] and of course in all the normative disciplines. In art he rejects deliberate attempts to separate **form** from the **matter** of experience. He makes his position abundantly clear in Part Four, Chapter XIX, of *Logic: The Theory of Inquiry,* which incidentally he entitles "the Logic of Scientific Method." In that specific chapter he distinguishes two different types of logical theory, the first of which maintains that forms constitute either metaphysical entities (he says "possibilities") or syntactical relations (of words in sentences). The opposed type of logical theory (his own) maintains the contrary view that forms are what he calls "forms-in-matter."[24]

As illustrations of the latter, he provides two sets of examples, one set dealing with legal forms and the other with aesthetic forms; but not entirely in separation from one another. He uses the legal examples to clarify by analogy the aesthetic examples. When reading Dewey it is always advisable to expect the unusual. Thus he says,

> No one has any doubt about the difference between this sort of [legal] form with respect to land [forms of record, seals, contractual requirements of offer, acceptance, & consideration, etc.] and that which makes a landscape an

22 Ibid., 140-41.
23 Ibid., 239.
24 Dewey, *Logic: The Theory of Inquiry,* 371-72.

esthetic object. Poetry is marked off from prosaic description by some special forms [e.g., rhythm & symmetry].[25]

Dewey does not deny that these imposed forms (either of a legal or aesthetic character) may exist independently of that which they inform or may be abstracted from that experiential matter, but the entity they aim at being or bringing into existence, e.g., a valid legal contract or a painted landscape, cannot exist without both, i.e., the form-in-matter. He summarizes as follows:

> That the material [of poetry and art generally, including architecture, etc.] existed independently of and prior to artistic treatment, and the relations by which that material takes on esthetic form . . . also exist independently, is undeniable. But it requires the deliberate effort which constitues art, and the deliberate efforts constituting the various arts, to bring the antecedent natural materials and relations together in the way that forms a work of art. The forms that result are capable of abstraction. As such they are the subject-matter of esthetic theory. But no one could construct a work of art out of the forms in isolation. Esthetic forms very definitely accrue to material in so far as materials are re-shaped to serve a definite purpose.[26]

Although adherence to aesthetic principles, both as guides for creative and decisive behavior, and as standards for judging art from non-art, and good art from bad, is fully consistent with the pragmatic perspective, despite Rorty's disagreement, still the perhaps "foolish" temptation, as Dewey puts it, to deviate from them still affects even the best public artists, including such persons as Thomas Jefferson, Frank Lloyd Wright, and Albert Speer.

---

25 Ibid.
26 Ibid., 374.

It may be instructive to examine how some of their deviations have produced difficulties and complexities.

Take, for example, Jefferson's penchant for oval rooms which he installed not only at Monticello, but also at Poplar Forest, and the Rotunda at the University of Virginia. The idea for oval rooms came to Jefferson not from Palladio but from his study of plates in Robert Morris' *Select Architecture*. His adoption of them was based on his thought that they provide better window placement and consequently better lighting. Although in those ways "convenient," it is also clear that they create difficulties. For example, if one places an oval within a square structure one is left with four oddly shaped spaces on the corners. Unless used as closets, as they usually are, they can amount to a significant loss of otherwise useable space. Even as closets the shelves are bound to be inefficiently triangular. Furthermore, oval rooms require curved walls and doors which add difficulties of construction, and undoubtedly increased costs. However, besides the benefit of better lighting, the ovals do often provide unexpected aesthetic pleasure.

The history of the design and development of Frank Lloyd Wright's *Fallingwater* is very enlightening regarding his employment and occasional abandonment of aesthetic and architectural principles. If Collingwood is right that no inquiry regarding the precise creative process is possible, we may not be able to grasp why, for example, Wright chose to place the house directly over the falls rather than, as had been customary in such situations, placing it beside the falls so that the falls could be viewed from the house itself. But other aspects of the artifact and its creation may be historically available to us and these we need to document.

E. J. Kaufmann, a wealthy Pittsburgh, Pennsylvania merchant, approached Wright regarding a summer weekend residence to be built in the Laurel Highlands, about 60 miles east of Pittsburgh, near a creek called "Bear Run." Like many other pragmatic architects before him, including Jefferson, he sought to integrate the structure into its natural environment. He sought also to maximize the lighting by a liberal use of glass, not only just below the ceilings with clerestory windows, but also entire walls in strategic locations. Furthermore there is no wasted space in the building. It is "teleological" in the sense that every window, wall, and bench serves some purpose. Decoration is minimized, but is not altogether absent because of his use of cubist and geometrical designs. His use of extensive overhangs and cantilevered floors and decks in all of his later buildings including *Fallingwater,* although not entirely original with Wright, were nonetheless very novel for the time and extensively copied later by Gropius and other members of the Bauhaus School of Architecture.[27]

Some disagreement exists among scholars as to whether Wright's use of glass and cantilevered construction was borrowed from such German architects as Gropius and Mies, and the Swiss-French architect, Le Corbusier, or whether they borrowed from Wright. In the specific case of *Fallingwater,* who borrowed from whom is at least arguable, but in general it appears that the Bauhaus and other European architects were greatly influenced initially by Wright who had published in 1910 & 1911 in Germany two portfolios of his buildings and projects, entitled *Augeführte Bauten und Entwürfe.* On the other hand, Gropius introduced the cantilevered glass wall which Wright at first objected to on the ground that it failed to reveal the structural support, and yet in *Fallingwater* he adopted a version of that notion. Obviously there was plagiarism on both sides.[28]

Wright was quite consistent in his adherence to the basic principles of pragmatic architecture,[29] but occasionally he did depart from those principles in certain significant ways. His engineering of the building's cantilevered structure was notoriously deficient as numerous later attempts to repair it have proved, and in this respect he departed markedly from what Toker calls his "structure based aesthetics."[30] Also, as one enters the

---

27   Cf. Franklin Toker, *Fallingwater Rising,* 22-23.

28   Wright was very much aware of his European competitors and regarded them as "enemies." Franklin Toker relates a story, told to him by a Taliesin apprentice, "that whenever Wright swatted flies . . . he would gleefully announce the window-kill as 'Got Gropius . . . got Mies . . . got Le Corbusier.'" *Fallingwter Rising,* 25.

29   Wright did briefly enunciate what he calls "the principles of organic architecture" in the publication, *The Natural House* (1954), the first principle of which is "Integration of the house and its site." For more on this specific but random discussion see Toker, *Fallingwater Rising,* 232, 442.

30   Toker, 22.

building one is immediately impressed by the relatively low ceilings, which, although intended to provide a sense of warmth and "convenience" in Jefferson's sense, seem to transmit the opposite feelings. Perhaps they are merely a reflection of the fact that Wright himself was not a tall person and did not feel the need for a more exalted space.

The overall aesthetic effect of *Fallingwater* as viewed particularly from the outside, however, is that it represents a deliberate and ingenious attempt to blend art with nature. That principally was what Wright was after in all his buildings, and he had little tolerance for criticisms based on merely mechanical features of construction. It was the artistic concept that mattered and little else, including costs and owner preferences[31]

That Albert Speer was intimately acquainted with the Palladian rules of classical architecture is suggested not only by his actual works but also by a remark he made regarding "Palladio's discovery of antiquity" in his diaries.[32] However, at some point during his Nuremburg trial and later in his reflections during his twenty years imprisonment at Spandau, it occurred to him that his lifelong commitment to classicism in architecture had perhaps been a mistake. As he wrote during his fifteenth year of imprisonment,

> The two great architectural forms, classicism and romanticism, which I always loved and as an architect unhesitatingly embraced, ultimately became a problem for me in a visibly increasing degree. I came to see their dangers more and more clearly—the dangers of perversion and of imitative atrophy. Romanticism ultimately turned into mere antagonism for civilization, a weakness for the pseudoprimitive, while classicism ended up in empty heroic bathos.[33]

---

31 Wright is famous for the cost overruns of his buildings, changing materials half-way through construction and ignoring owner protests.

32 Speer, *Spandau: The Secret Diaries*, 399.

33 Ibid., 398-99.

It is not altogether clear what exactly he means by "the great architectural form of romanticism," although presumably it was the trend during the eighteenth and early nineteenth centuries toward the introduction of "exotic" elements such as "paraphrases" of Egyptian temples, oriental roofs, Chinese latticework, Swiss chalet styles, etc. Outside Berlin and other major cities in Germany, Speer did indulge himself by incorporating such features in country homes and other buildings. But it is also clear that he came to regard such "romantic" characteristics as "imitative" and "antagonistic toward civilization," which is somewhat strange, coming from a man who at least passively, and at least in some respect actively, supported one of the most uncivilized regimes the world has ever known! But it is also clear that he came to regard his (and Hitler's) penchant toward classicism as leading to "empty heroic bathos."

Although Speer even while in prison, by reading architectural magazines, was well acquainted with contemporary architecture and especially with the Bauhaus style as represented by the work of Gropius and Mies even after they migrated to the United States, and also with the work of Le Corbusier. He shows, however, no indication that he thought that architecture should move in that direction. He appears to have retained his appreciation of classicism as the premier style. His reference to its leading to "empty heroic bathos" must not be understood as a sheer rejection of classicism, but only of his former megalomaniac version of it. Indeed he often regretted his subservience to Hitler's love of monstrous buildings, but nonetheless went along with his wishes. Quite obviously Speer came to realize that his "perverse" departure from what he had been taught by his teacher, Tessenow, and the views of his own father,[34] was a vast, tragic, but unforgivable error.

---

34 Cf. Speer, *Spandau,* 74, 412.

Chapter XI

IS AESTHETIC VALUE SUPERIOR TO MORAL VALUE? IS BEING AESTHETICALLY RIGHT PREFERABLE TO BEING MORALLY RIGHT? DOES ART ALWAYS TRUMP MORALITY?

The exact relationship between art and morality and their respective fields of philosophical investigation, aesthetics and ethics, has been long debated. Essentially there are three positions. The first is what might be called the "Separatist" view that art and morality, aesthetic value and moral value, aesthetics and ethics are totally distinct from one another and ought never to be confused. Art is art, morality is morality, and never the twain shall meet. What passes for art, whether good or bad, is one kind of reality; what passes for morality or moral conduct is quite another. As we shall see, Clive Bell expresses just such a view, although with a significant qualification.

The second theory has been called the "Moralistic" view. It is perhaps the most popular view among art observers and possibly also among art critics. It is the view that art is subordinate to morality, or put another way, legitimate or "real" art must always serve the interests of morality. If a work of art depicts sexual deviance, obscene behavior, pornography, or disrespect for customary mores, it must be condemned and made illegal. How often have United States Senators and other Congressional representatives expressed their disapproval of certain works of arts shown to the public by public museums; how often do we hear a call for a cancellation of funds for The National Endowment for the Arts and/or the National Endowment for the Humanities, even demanding their total abolition? In their view, the State has no business supporting such "degenerate" art. Hitler, of course, is the extreme example of this moralistic view, but he has not been alone. Many others, holding quite different moral perspectives have also judged aesthetics as subordinate to ethics, and aesthetic value inferior to moral value. Jacques Maritain, for example, expressing a strictly Thomistic point of view, has said in his book, *The Responsibility of the Artist,*

> And because an artist is a man before being an artist, the autonomous world of morality is simply superior to (and more inclusive than) the autonomous world of art. There is no law against the law[on] which the destiny of man depends. In other words, art is indirectly and extrinsically subordinate to morality.[1]

The third position may be called the "Aesthetic" theory. André Gide, in response to the question, "But what is morality to you? is reported to have said, 'A branch of Aesthetics.'" Another way of expressing this view is in terms of style. Thus A. N. Whitehead has said, "Style is the ultimate morality of the mind."[2] R. G. Collingwood has also expressed the view that "Subject without style is barbarism; style without subject is dilettantism. Art is the two together." [3] Both of these latter views stress the supreme importance of aesthetic style. John Dewey bases his appreciation of art and aesthetic experience in part at least on his critique of our closed-minded, self-righteous theory of moral blameworthiness. William James finds that "many of the so-called metaphysical [moral and even scientific] principles are at bottom only expressions of aesthetic feeling."[4] Whitehead cites similar considerations to account for the rise and development of science in the

---

1 Maritain, *The Responsibility of the Artist,* Ch. I, § 4.
2 Whitehead, *The Aims of Education,* 24.
3 Collingwood, *The Principles of Art,* 299.
4 James, "Aesthetic and Moral Principles," in PP-II, ch. xxviii, 672.

modern world.[5] In general, pragmatists, with important qualifications and modifications, seem to gravitate toward this third position regarding the relation of art to matters of morality. But let us examine each of them in closer detail.

In Bell's view, the "world of man's activity" is sharply distinguished from the "world of esthetic exaltation" in which the "emotions of life" play no role since it has "emotions of its own." [6] Given such an absolute dichotomy it is obvious that what obtains in our world (the world of moral action) is totally distinct from what obtains in the other (the world of art). Thus it should not surprise anyone who holds such a view that an artist could be the worst person in the (active) world, and yet be a superlative artist. Indeed, this circumstance seems to be well substantiated by actual fact. Think of how many great musicians, painters, sculptors, and architects have private lives which leave much to be desired morally.[7] Aristotle long ago drew a distinction between two kinds of virtue, intellectual and moral. He clearly saw that a person might be excellent (i.e. virtuous) in the performance of his trade or occupation and yet be deficient in the moral realm (i.e. lack virtue in the moral sense). Bell and all others who believe that artistic talent is inborn and incapable of being learned in the usual way could easily adopt such a perspective: Let only the artistically superior judge art; leave morality to the moralist, but keep his hands off art!

Bell does allow one important qualification of his view, however. Although he holds steadfastly to the view that "art is above morals," or alternatively that "all art is moral," (24) and that a person's "moral judgments about the value of particular works of art have nothing to do with their artistic value," (84) still he maintains that significant (i.e., genuine) art works are "immediate means to good." As he puts it, "Once we have judged a thing a work of art, we have judged it ethically of the first importance and put it beyond the reach of the moralist." (24)

---

5   Whitehead, *Science and the Modern World,* 12-13, 196-200.

6   Bell, cf. below, 76. All subsequent quotations of Bell are documented parenthetically in the text.

7   To mention only one case: Frank Lloyd Wright, whose private life and individual genius became the plot of Ayn Rand's novel, *The Fountainhead.*

Another way he expresses his idea of the relation of morals to art is in terms of the concept of right. An artist, he maintains, must always aim at making his work of art "right." In a way reminiscent of Dewey he defines right to mean "aesthetically satisfying, i.e. the complete realisation of a conception, a perfect solution of a problem." (52). Jefferson too often speaks of getting works of architecture "right and beautiful," usually meaning, however, complete conformity to Palladian rules. Bell attaches a somewhat more explicitly moral meaning to the term right when he later says,

> When you treat a picture as a work of art, you have, unconsciously perhaps, made a far more important moral judgment. . . Paradoxical as it may seem, the only relevant qualities in a work of art, judged as art, are artistic qualities: judged as a means to good, no other qualities are worth considering: for there are no qualities of greater moral value than artistic qualities since there is no greater means to good than art. (84-5)

Bell, and possibly also Dewey, in this respect appear to have confused aesthetic rightness with moral rightness. Da Vinci's *Mona Lisa* can be said to be "aesthetically right" and indeed a contribution without which the world would be a sorrier place, but in what clearly understandable sense can it be said to be morally right?[8] Bell's view also suggests that somehow the realms of art and morals are coextensive, but as Maritain points out, that is not true. The moral realm far exceeds the artistic realm. Nor does it make any obvious sense to say that "there are no qualities of greater moral value than artistic qualities." Are honor and justice of lesser value than picturesqueness and beauty? Many persons, particularly many philosophers, including Plato and Jefferson, would certainly disagree.

---

8 It could of course be maintained, as Bell indeed would, that making the world a better place is a moral judgment about rightness, but there are many great works of art—some very dreary, depressing, even revolting—of which that judgment could not be made.

In direct opposition to this separatist point of view (which seems less and less consistently separatist when one adds in Bell's qualification), is the moralistic view which holds, on the contrary, that moral values are superior to aesthetic values, or to put it in terms of "rightness," that moral righteousness is superior to aesthetic righteousness (or rightness). The moralist does not say, as Bell does, that to "pronounce anything a work of art is to make a momentous moral judgment" (84), but he or she does maintain that moral judgments can always be made regarding any work of art. Aesthetic value is always subordinate to moral value.

There are several problems with this view even if we agree that all human acts and artifacts are subject to moral evaluation. First whose moral standards are to be used? Second, must all art serve some moral end or purpose, and if not, are moral judgments of art really necessary? Third, if objective moral judgments of art are possible, can some arts be judged morally and aesthetically superior to other arts, e.g., can architecture be judged superior to sculpture, or drama superior in moral status to music?

To answer these questions in reverse order. Arthur Schopenhauer thought that music was the highest art form, a view with which Richard Wagner disagreed. The latter thought that opera represented what he called *Gesamtkunstwerk*, or a "total work of art," in which music is subordinated to drama. Undoubtedly others have made similar comparative judgments. Jefferson, for example, often speaks of architecture as an "eloquent" art, so presumably in his view there are other not-so-eloquent arts.

It is perfectly true that in many normative disciplines we make comparative value judgments. For example, in law we distinguish petty larceny from grand larceny; in morals, we distinguish white lies from heinous ones, and truths from prevarications; and in economics, fair dealing from deceitful or conspiratorial practices. But except when their subjects overlap (as often they do because they all deal with human actions), we do not judge them comparatively; that is, we do not say that a marriage counselor's job (as a moralist) is inferior to that of a judge or a business executive; nor do we judge a lawyer's occupation or actions as superior to that of a preacher's. We do judge murder as worse than manslaughter, and life saving (in some circumstances) as better than truth telling, but these are all comparative judgments within a given discipline, not so to speak, "cross-disciplinary" judgments.

And that is the trouble with judgments that music is superior to drama, or architecture superior to sculpture. These judgments are akin to comparing apples to oranges. Or perhaps a better analogy is the attempt to pick a "best of show" animal at kennel exhibitions of various breeds of dogs. Certainly one can reasonably compare dogs within a given breed, but really what sense does it make to compare a Pekinese to a Bloodhound? That is about as sensible as insisting that a Picasso painting is better (in a moral or any other sense) than the Taj Mahal or the Golden Gate Bridge.[9] The salient point is that those art works are simply not comparable, and to suppose otherwise contributes nothing but confusion.

But why make any moral judgments about art at all? Why not simply treat art as a special case of human activity and let artists do as they please without attempts to evaluate their work? The answer to that question seems to be that unless one is prepared to countenance irrationality by denying the possibility or advisability of making any objective judgments about art, it would appear not merely possible but necessary to do so. The reason that it is necessary is that art itself is as necessary for human existence as is water, food, and shelter. And just as it is necessary to have these latter things evaluated to make sure that they are not inimical to us, we must make judgments about artworks. One might doubt this claim that art in this respect is on a par with food, water, and shelter, but try to imagine a life totally without art. Even the cavemen required drawings on the walls of their caves. Consider also the fact which has frequently been verified that prisoners put in solitary confinement in stark environments for long periods of time go mad. A life without art of any sort would be a nightmare.

---

9 The usual justification given for the comparisons made at Kennel Shows is that, on the contrary, all that is being compared is the extent to which each subject has achieved excellence in its own field, but of course that is as much a judgment regarding the trainer or the breeder as it is the qualities of the dog, and is rarely understood by the public in that manner.

Even if this claim about the necessity of art and the consequent necessity of art criticism is accepted,[10] there is still another problem facing the moralistic theory, and that concerns whose moral standards are to be employed in evaluating art. Should they be the standards of some U. S. Senator, some dictator such as Hitler, someone persuaded by Utilitarianism or by Immanuel Kant, some survivalist principle, the Golden Rule, or is it the case, as William James says, "No single abstract principle can be so used as to yield to the philosopher anything like a scientifically accurate and genuinely useful casuistic scale"? And we might add, "any useful rule by which to judge aesthetic value."

John Dewey, who leans decidedly toward the Aesthetic Theory of the relation of morality and art in his books, *Art As Experience*[11] and *Human Nature and* Conduct, is another who would agree with James. He bases his aesthetic theory at least in part on his criticism of our society's usual practice of blaming wrongdoers for their misdeeds and at the same time failing to admit that we, or society, are co-partners in their wrongs. As he puts it:

> Our entire tradition regarding punitive justice tends to prevent recognition of social partnership in producing crime. . . By killing an evil-doer or shutting him up behind stone walls, we are enabled to forget both him and our part in creating him.[12]

He objects to the "abstract theory of justice which demands the 'vindication' of law irrespective of [the] instruction and reform of the wrong-doer,"[13] and insists that in such situations "distinctly personal or subjective factors" be taken into account; in other words, aesthetic considerations. Otherwise,

---

10   Clive Bell for one has said, "Art is, in fact, a necessity to and a product of the spiritual life." *Art*, 59. Whitehead, for another, says that "fertilization of the soul is the reason for the necessity of art." *Science and the Modern World*, 202.

11   Dewey, *Art As Experience*, 39.

12   Dewey, *Human Nature and Conduct*, 18

13   Ibid., 22.

as he expresses the point elsewhere,[14] we are left with an *anesthetic* morality, which leads only to worse and even more irrational consequences.

Dewey is by no means suggesting that by taking such subjective factors into account we are trying to make "a suffering victim out of the criminal." That would be as bad as unthinkingly putting all the blame on him for his wrongs. But he does suggest that our system of justice should allow, as at times it does, the dispensation of mercy and open-mindedness about the crime and its perpetrator. Dewey does not use the term "open-mindedness"[15] in this connection, but he does say, speaking metaphorically, "A genuine appreciation of the beauty of flowers is not generated within a self-enclosed consciousness."[16]

Besides finding that many moral and scientific principles, such as the principle that the truth is knowable; that nature repeats itself (i.e., the principle of the uniformity of nature); that simplicity in natural laws is desirable; that promise keeping is of the highest value; that all events have causes, etc., are regularly based on seldom admitted aesthetic preferences,[17] James sums up his view of the relations between feelings and ideas, at the very beginning rather than at the end of his essay, *On a Certain Blindness in Human Beings:*

> Our judgments concerning the worth of things, big or little, depend on the *feelings* the things arouse in us. Where we judge a thing to be precious in consequence of the *idea* we frame of it, this is only because the idea is itself associated already with a feeling. If we were radically feelingless, and if ideas were the only things our mind could entertain, we should lose all our likes and dislikes at a stroke, and be

---

14   Dewey, *Art As Experience,* "One great defect in what passes for morality is its anesthetic quality." 39. Cf. James also, "The Sentiment of Rationality," 64, 107.

15   As James frequently does to describe the pragmatic spirit and perspective. James even dedicated his book, *Pragmatism,* "To the memory of John Stuart Mill from whom I first learned the pragmatic openness of mind."

16   Dewey, *Human Nature and Conduct,"* 22.

17   See particularly the following essays by James: *The Sentiment of Rationality, The Will to Believe,* and *The Moral Philosopher and the Moral Life.*

unable to point to any one situation or experience in life more valuable or significant than any other.[18]

For expressing just such statements about the role of feelings and other personal and subjective factors in human life, James has been dubbed "the quintessential emotional philosopher" by his biographer, Gerald E. Myers,[19] and his views regarding what constitutes rationality interpreted by many others as nothing more than an exhortation of sentimentalism. But these views appear to be mistaken not only with respect to James who, as we have already seen,[20] emphatically rejects the kind of sentimentalism expressed by the English couple who spent hours emoting over Titian's painting, *Assumption,*"but also with respect to Dewey who explicitly disapproves of any "sentimental gush which makes a suffering victim out of a criminal."[21] When James speaks of the "sentiment of rationality" he is not, as we have also seen,[22] referring to what Wright calls "sheer ordinary" and "invidious" sentiments, but to a kind of thinking that is quite different from such feelings as well as different from formal abstract thought of the syllogistic variety.

What James is promoting, and Dewey as well, is a new definition of what it means to be rational. They are convinced that the traditional and academically accepted ways of thinking are not the only ways. Collingwood, as we have seen,[23] shares this view. All of these philosophers agree that on many occasions and in certain situations it is inappropriate and grossly in error to ignore personal and subjective, indeed aesthetic, considerations. Thus, Dewey is of the opinion that it is far from rational to hold a wrongdoer wholly blameworthy and responsible for an act which society has had a hand in producing, and that in such a situation it is preeminently rational to extend mercy and perhaps even forgiveness. James too points out that

---

18 James, *On a Certain Blindness in Human Beings,* 259.
19 Myers, *William James: His Life and Thought,* 49
20 James, below, 22.
21 Dewey, *Human Nature and Conduct,* 17.
22 Cf. Wright, below, 96, 99.
23 Collingwood, *The Principles of Art,* 287.

according to the Principle of Utility, one consequence of its use might be the suppression of the rights of a minority in order to maximize happiness for the majority. If, as he says, "millions [could be] kept permanently happy on the one simple condition that a certain lost soul on the far-oof edge of things should lead a life of lonely torture . . . how hideous a thing [aestheticlly speaking] would be its enjoyment when deliberately accepted as the fruit of such a bargain?"[24] And in what sense rational? Or consider the supposed rationality of Kant's purely legalistic view that lying even to save a life is immoral, and his judgment that in the hypothetical case of a society forced by circumstances to dissolve itself, all duly convicted criminals should be executed rather than freed and consequently released from the strict application of the laws."[25] How utterly appalling! And how unspeakably irrational! No pragmatist could possibly accept such a view.

On the contrary, according to the pragmatic perspective, the concept of rationality must always include respect for certain personal and subjective considerations—in other words aesthetic considerations. In law, Justice Oliver Wendell Holmes, speaking generally to judges, advises them to be sure to include in their deliberations "considerations of social advantage," and that the use of force be "tempered by sympathy and all the social feelings."[26] Without these kinds of aesthetic considerations, disastrous result occur. In law we get what Roscoe Pound and others call "mechanical jurisprudence;" in ethics, what both James and Dewey describe as "anesthetic" or "paralytic" morality."[27]

If a more theoretical or ontological rationale for this relatively novel pragmatic theory of rationality is required, James supplies one with his theory of the "whole man." According to James,

> It is utterly hopeless to try to exorcise such sensitiveness by
> calling it the disturbing subjective factor, and branding it

---

24 James, "the Moral Philosopher and the Moral Life," 188.
25 Cf. Kant, "Theory and Practice," and *Rechtslehre* or *Science of Right*.
26 For more on Holmes' view see *The Common Law*, 38; also Davis, *Comparative Philosophy*, Ch.. VII, "The Logic of Choice: Holmes on Decisions, James on Belief."
27 See James, "The Sentiment of Rationality," 64, 107, 94; Dewey, *Art As Experience*, 39.

as the root of all evil. 'Subjective' be it called! and 'disturb-ing' to those it foils! But if it helps . . . it is good and not evil. Pretend what we may, *the whole man* within us is at work when we form our philosophical opinions. Intellect, will, taste, and passion co-operate just as they do in practi-cal affairs.[28]

And in a passage with an even larger scope, and implicitly including aes-thetics as well as science and philosophy, he says,

> Every philosopher, or man of science either, whose initiative counts for anything in the evolution of thought, has taken his stand on a sort of dumb conviction that the truth must lie in one direction rather than another. . . These mental instincts in different men are the spontaneous variations upon which the intellectual struggle for existence is based. . . . The concrete man [presumably the artist as well] has but one interest—to be right. That for him is the art of all arts.[29]

By insisting that aesthetic considerations infiltrate our moral as well as our scientific notions and judgments, are James and other pragmatists such as Dewey in effect agreeing with Separatists such as Clive Bell regard-ing the relation of art to morality? The answer seems to be no, primarily because the pragmatist does not mean to separate the reality of art from the reality of morality, but to integrate the two without depriving morality of its distinctive function as a critic of artistic products. Is the pragmatic position then that of the Moralist, e.g., Jacques Maritain, who holds that aesthetics is always subordinate to ethics, and art to morality? Again the answer is no, because from the perspective of pragmatism the moralistic view lacks "openness of mind," and settles upon dogmatic conclusions just

---

28 James, "The Sentiment of Rationality," 92. Italics mine.
29 James, Ibid., 93.

as Utilitarians and Marxists do regarding the ultimate goals of society. No general criterion can be applied to all artistic creations, whether they be the visual arts or architecture. Their value must be assessed only upon their completion and the extent to which they contribute to the betterment and well-being of the human world. In short, the moralistic view lacks open-endedness as well as open-mindedness and so pragmatists oppose it.

Are pragmatists, and like-minded philosophers such as A. N. Whitehead and R. G. Collingwood with their views about aesthetic style, of the alternative opinion that art always trumps morality? This too is a mistaken view. Pragmatists, Whitehead, and Collingwood not only wish, by their adoption of a more inclusive and humane notion of rationality, to enhance both art and morality. They not only wish to provide some objective basis for rational judgments about art, but to permit risk taking not only in matters of scientific and philosophical belief but also in artistic creation. James puts it supremely well when he says,

> The ultimate philosophy . . . must not be too strait-laced in form, must not in all its parts divide heresy from orthodoxy by too sharp a line. There must be left over and above the propositions to be subscribed . . . another realm into which the stifled soul may escape from pedantic scruples and indulge its own faith at its own risks.[30]

---

30 James, Ibid, 110.

REFERENCES

Adams, William Howard, *Jefferson's Monticello*. N.Y. : Abbeville Press, 1983.

Alexander, Thomas M., *John Dewey's Theory of Art, Experience, and Nature: The Horizons of Feeling*. Albany: SUNY, 1987.

Aristotle, *Poetics,* in *The Basic Works of Aristotle,* ed. Richard McKeon. N.Y.: Random House, 1941.

Bacon, Francis, *Essays and New Atlantis,* ed. Gordon S. Haight. N.Y.: Van Nostrand, 1942.

Beasley, Sandra, "American Idol." *The Washington Post Magazine.* Nov. 15, 2009.

Bell, Clive, *Art.* N.Y.: Capricorn Books, 1958.

Beeman, Richard R., *Patrick Henry, A Biography.* N.Y.: McGraw-Hill, 1974.

Collingwood, *The Principles of Art.* Oxford: Oxford U. Press, 1935/1958.

_____, *The Idea of History,* N.Y.: Oxford U. Press, 1956.

Cruel, James Stevens, *A Dictionary of Architecture.* Oxford: Oxford U. Press, 1999.

Davis, Philip E., *Comparative Philosophy: Four Philosophical Americans.* North Charleston: Create-Space, 2014.

_____, *The Philosophy of Place.* North Charleston: Create-Space, 2014.

_____, *The Scalping of the Great Sioux Nation.* Lanham, Maryland: Hamilton Books, 2010.

DeVoto, Bernard, *Mark Twain's America.* Boston: Moscow, Idaho: U. of Idaho Press, 1932.

_____, ed., *The Portable Mark Twain.* N.Y.: Viking, 1968.

Dewey, John, *Art As Experience.* N.Y.: Perigee Books, 1934/1980.

_____, *Experience and Nature.* N.Y.: Dover, 1958.

_____, *Human Nature and Conduct.* N.Y.: Modern Library, 1922/1930

_____, *Logic: The Theory of Inquiry.* N.Y.: Henry Holt, 1938.

Foner, Philip S., *Mark Twain: Social Critic,* N.Y.: International Publishers, 1972.

Haines, John, *Living Off the Country: Essays on Poetry and Places.* Ann Arbor: U. of Michigan Press, 1981.

Hegel, G. W. F., *Lectures on the Philosophy of World History,* tr. Johannes Hoffmeister. N.Y.: Cambridge U. Press, 1975.

Hitler, Adolf, *Mein Kampf,* The Ford Translation. Elite-Minds Inc.: 2009/2010.

Holmes, Oliver Wendell, Jr., *The Common Law,* ed. Mark DeWolfe Howe. Boston: Little, Brown & Co. 1963.

_____, "The Gas Stokers Strike"" in Lerner, 48.

_____, "The Path of the Law," in Lerner, 71.

Hospers, John, *Meaning and Truth in the Arts.* Chapel Hill: U. of Carolina Press, 1946.

Isaacson, Walter, *Einstein: His Life and Universe.* N.Y.: Simon and Schuster, 2007.

James, William, *The Correspondence of William James,* ed. Ignas Skrupskelis & Elizabeth Berkeley. Charlottesville: U. Press of Virginia, vol. III.

_____, *Essays on Faith and Morals.* N.Y.: Longmans, Green & Co., 1949.

_____, *Pragmatism: A New Name For Some Old Ways of Thinking,* N.Y.: Longmans, Green & Co., 1947.

_____, *The Principles of Psychology,* vol. II. N.Y.: Dover, 1950.

_____, *Psychology: The Briefer Course.* N.Y.: Henry Holt, 1920.

Jefferson, Thomas, *Notes on the State of Virginia.* ed. William Peden. N.Y.: Norton, 1954.

Kant, Immanuel, "Theory and Practice: Concerning the Common Saying: This May Be True in Theory But Does Not Apply to Practice." in *The Philosophy of Kant: Immanuel Kant's Moral and Political Writings.* ed. Carl Friedrich.. N.Y.: Modern Library, 1949.

_____, *Fundamental Principles of the Metaphysics of Morals,* tr. T.K. Abbott. N.Y.: Liberal Arts Press, 1949.

_____, *The Science of Right (Rechtslehre),* tr. W. Hastie.

Kemmis, Daniel, *Community and the Politics of Place.* Norman: U. of Oklahoma Press, 1990.

Kimball, Fiske, *Thomas Jefferson Architect.* Boston:, 1916, reprinted with Intro. By Frederick D. Nichols, DeCapo Press, 1968.

Kuhn, Thomas S., *The Structure of Scientific Revolutions.* Chicago: U. of Chicago Press, 1996.

Leddy, Thomas, *The Extraordinary in the Ordinary: The Aesthetics of Everyday Life.* Peterborough, Canada: Broadview Press, 2012.

Lennard, Suzanne H. Crowhurst, *Explorations in the Meanings of Architecture.* Woodstock, N.Y.: Gondolier Press, 1979.

_____, "A House is a Metaphor" in *Journal of Architectural Education.* XXVII, No. 2, 3, June, 1974.

Lerner, Max, *The Mind and Faith of Justice Holmes.* N.Y.: Modern Library, 1943.

Malone, Dumas, *Jefferson The President: First Term, 1801-1805.* Little, Brown & Co., 1970.

Maritain, Jacques, *The Responsibility of the Artist.* Princeton: Princeton U. Press, 1960.

Matthiessen, F. O., *The James Family: A Group Biography.* N.Y.: Knopf, 1947.

McLaughlin, Jack, *Jefferson and Monticello: The Biography of a Builder.* N.Y.: Henry Holt, 1988.

Myers, Gereald E., *William James: His Life and Thought.* New Haven: Yale U. Press, 1986.

Palladio, Andrea, *Quatro Libri dell'Architettura* (The Four Books). 1570.

Peterson, Merrill D., ed. *Jefferson Writings.* N.Y.: Library of America, 1984. (All references to Jefferson's letters are to this collection, unless specified otherwise.)

Plato, *Apology of Socrates,* tr. Hugh Trudennick in *The Collected Dialogues of Plato,* ed. Edith Hamilton & Huntington Cairns. N.Y.: Bollingen Foundation, 1961.

Rorty, Richard, *Achieving Our Country.* Cambridge: Harvard, 1998.

_____, *Consequences of Pragmatism*. Minneapolis: U. of Minnesota Press, 1982/ 1994.

_____, *Philosophy and Social Hope*. London: Penguin Books, 1999.

Rasmusser, William M. S. & Tilton, Robert S., *George Washington: the Man Behind the Myths*. Charlottesville: U. Press of Virginia, 1999.

Schilpp, Paul Arthur, ed. *The Philosophy of John Dewey*. Evanston: Northwestern U., 1939.

Speer, Albert, *Inside the Third Reich*. N.Y.: Collier Books, 1970.

_____, *Spandau: The Secret Diaries*. N.Y.: Pocket Books, 1976.

Thayer, H. S., *Pragmatism: The Classical Writings*. Indianapolis: Hackett, 1982.

Toker, Franklin, *Fallingwater Rising*. N.Y.: Knopf, 2003.

Vitruvius Pollo, Marcus, *De Architectura*. 1771 (first English tr. of first five books) ; 1791 (second English tr. of whole treatise).

White, Morton G., *A Philosophy of Culture: The Scope of Holistic Pragmatism*. Princeton: Princeton U. Press, 2002.

Whitehead, Alfred North, *The Aims of Education and Other Essays*. N.Y.: Mentor, 1953.

_____, *Process and Reality*. N.Y.: Social Science Book Store, 1929.

_____, *Science and the Modern World*. N.Y.: The Free Press, 1925/ 1967.

Westbrook, Robert B., *John Dewey and American Democracy*. Ithaca: Cornel U. Press, 1991.

Wright, Frank Lloyd, *Ausgeführte Bauten und Entwürfe* (Two portfolios of his buildings and projects). Germany, 1910, 1911.

_____, *An Autobiography*. Portland, OR.: Pomegranate Communications, 2005.

INDEX

Made in the USA
Charleston, SC
25 June 2015